Neutrality and
Foreign Military Sales

Neutrality and Foreign Military Sales

Military Production and Sales Restrictions in Austria, Finland, Sweden, and Switzerland

Björn Hagelin

Westview Press
BOULDER, SAN FRANCISCO, & OXFORD

This Westview softcover edition is printed on acid-free paper and bound in library-quality, coated covers that carry the highest rating of the National Association of State Textbook Administrators, in consultation with the Association of American Publishers and the Book Manufacturers' Institute.

Copyright © 1990 by Westview Press, Inc.

Published in 1990 in the United States of America by Westview Press, Inc., 5500 Central Avenue, Boulder, Colorado 80301, and in the United Kingdom by Westview Press, Inc., 36 Lonsdale Road, Summertown, Oxford OX2 7EW

Library of Congress Cataloging-in-Publication Data
Hagelin, Björn, 1947– .
Neutrality and foreign military sales: military production and
sales restrictions in Austria, Finland, Sweden, and Switzerland/by
Björn Hagelin.
    p. cm.
Includes bibliographical references.
ISBN 0-8133-7928-8
    1. Munitions—Europe—Case studies. 2. Military assistance—Case
studies. 3. Austria—Neutrality. 4. Finland—Neutrality.
5. Sweden—Neutrality. 6. Switzerland—Neutrality. I. Title.
HD9743.E922H34 1990
382′.456234′094—dc20   89-48381
                                                              CIP

Printed and bound in the United States of America

∞ The paper used in this publication meets the requirements
    of the American National Standard for Permanence of Paper
    for Printed Library Materials Z39.48-1984.

10   9   8   7   6   5   4   3   2   1

Contents

Figures and Tables

Figures

Tables

Appendix Tables

Acknowledgments

In late 1984 a number of individuals from Austria, Finland, Sweden and Switzerland met at the Austrian Peace Research Institute (APRI) in Stadtschlaining, Burg. They agreed to pursue a research project about the European neutrals following national and international debates about their foreign military sales. Quite naturally, the Austrian participants were in the majority: Wilfrid Graf, Walter Lauber, Josef Binter (who hosted the meeting), Karl Wörister, Arno Truger and Peter Pilz. Finland was represented by Pertti Joenniemi, the originator of the idea, Jouko Huru and Arto Kosonen. The present author (Sweden) and Rudolf Wullschleger from Switzerland completed the group. A special thanks goes to Josef Binter and the APRI for the excellent arrangements and financial support.

Three preliminary national case studies were presented at the second meeting in Switzerland by Peter Pilz from Austria, Pertti Joenniemi from Finland, and the present author. One person who deserves our full appreciation is Rudolf Wullschleger. Not only did he cover part of the costs and arrange the meeting at the Trigon-Institut in Zurich, but he also invited the Swiss members: Toni Bernet, Peter Hug and Jakob Tanner. It fell upon Peter Hug to write the Swiss case study.

A third meeting was arranged by the Tampere Peace Research Institute (TAPRI), Finland, in the Spring of 1987. Peter Pilz had by then been elected representative of the Austrian Green Party and could therefore not devote more time to the project. Arno Truger shouldered the responsibility for continuing the Austrian part of the project.

The present study would have involved much more hardship had I not had access to the mentioned unpublished and later updated case studies, the additional information supplied by individual group members and the financial support from external sources. I regret that I have not been able to use all of the information collected by the group. The Nordic Cooperation Committee for International Politics including Conflict and Peace Research, Stockholm, made it possible for me to attend most of the group meetings. The Committee also supported a trip to Tampere in the Fall of 1987. Most importantly, throughout the project Professor Peter Wallensteen and Associate Professor Mats Hammarström, Department of Peace and Conflict Research at Uppsala University, gave me invaluable comments and advice. Ms. Karin Lindgren, supported by a grant from the Nordic Cooperation Committee, saved me from the tedious task of compiling several years of statistical information from the Swedish National Bureau of Statistics. I am also grateful for suggestions on parts of the final manuscript by Dr. Wilhelm Agrell, Lund University, and Mr. Rickard Holm, Uppsala University. With the assistance of Mr. Göran Lindgren at the Department of Peace and Conflict Research the computer became my friend. Last, but not least, Jeanne Campbell, Michelle Starika and Jan Kristiansson at Westview Press corrected and edited the final text.

Nevertheless, I am solely responsible for the way the material is presented and for the conclusions drawn.

Björn Hagelin
Uppsala, Sweden

1

Introduction

Is there anything peculiar about neutrality apart from formal non-alignment in peacetime and the attempt to stay neutral in wartime? If so, what is it? These questions are as old as they are controversial (for reasons of simplicity the terms *non-alignment* and *neutrality* are used as synonymus in describing the general peacetime policy). On the one hand governments of neutral countries argue that neutrality is a peace-supporting and stabilizing policy in a world dominated by major-power politics. Representatives of alliance members, on the other hand, are not late to respond that 'peace', meaning primarily the avoidance of a 'hot' East-West war in Europe after 1945, is the result of the two super-power alliances and their deterrent effects. From this point of view nuclear weapons and their 'mutually assured destruction' have secured peace through fear. In such a bipolar view of the world, neutrality may even be regarded as a destabilizing policy.

There is also the argument that neutrality as such is not a viable alternative in a future war in Europe. The reason is not only that a future war is assumed by many to be, or to quickly become, an all-out nuclear conflict with no survivors. The reason is also that the neutrals in Europe, all of them small countries, are not seen by the critics to pursue a strictly neutral policy. Instead, because of the strong dependence of the neutrals upon international trade in general, and upon trade with the Western industrialized countries in particular, their foreign and security policies are also assumed to be biased. Neutrality therefore seems a theoretical policy with no place in the real world of international dependence, global power politics and welfare economics. In short, to the critics, neutrality is not a credible wartime policy.

2

Introduction

But neutrality is just as much, if not even more so, a peacetime policy. It might even be called peaceful. Armed solutions to political, ethnic, religious and other sources of conflict should not be supported. This view has lead to a particular neutral dilemma, which was very strongly exposed during the 1970s and 1980s, when the bigger European neutrals – Austria, Finland, Sweden and Switzerland – started making headlines for their foreign military sales. Whereas until then the neutrals had generally been known for restrictive military sales policies, they were now recognized for their increasing sales, especially to poor countries or regions of the world.

Contrary to previous national debates about foreign military sales, the issue did not quickly disappear. This has been particularly evident in Sweden. Before, debates had generally been *ad hoc* dealing with individual cases of military sales. The debates had been as short or as long as the public and media interest permitted, which in general was not very long. This time, however, new deals – both legal and illegal – came to the surface, partly through 'investigative journalism'. Some of these cases created big question marks as to the involvement of military firms, governments and individuals. Foreign military sales, not individual cases, were taken up as a political issue by itself with consequences for neutrality as a legitimate policy and national armament as a solution to national security. More public and academic interest arose around the issue. The public as well as political groups and individuals demanded and suggested changes of policy, ranging from an unconditional embargo on all foreign military sales to a more liberal (according to some more 'realistic') foreign military sales policy.

Neutrality as such was at the center of at least one of the suggested solutions, namely, that the neutrals should increase military sales among themselves in an attempt to reduce their global military trade. Such a 'directed' foreign military sales policy seems first to have been formulated in the mid-1980s by the Swedish Ecumenical Council. It has since then been incorporated into a more comprehensive ecumenical peace policy proposal (*Fredspolitik för 90-talet* 1989). The idea, which also encompasses the Nordic countries, has been taken up by other groups. The Swedish Prime Minister in September of 1986 supported the idea during a visit to Bofors, one of the main Swedish military producers (*N-Syntesen* 1986, no. 5, p. 4).

One of the ambitions of this book is to discuss whether such an alternative is possible and, if so, what it could possibly look like. But first, let us look at some of the more general issues involved.

1.1 THE LARGER ISSUES

The issue of foreign military sales is related to important aspects of neutral foreign policy. The most crucial aspects can be summarized as 'the L's, the A's and the R'. They make up what is here called the LAR pyramid (figure 1.1).

It is probably uncontroversial to suggest that the neutrals *want* to appear special, even if it is not always possible to distinguish the finer day-to-day differences between the foreign policy of a neutral and the foreign policies of most other nations. When trying to do so, however, some issues appear more important than others. Perhaps most important of all is *Law*, here understood as international law. Without the respect for international law, neutrality is very much a policy without a meaning. This is particularly so for Austria and Switzerland, which have neutrality policies founded in international agreements. This is not the case for Finland and Sweden. Sweden has pursued a self-defined neutrality policy since the early nineteenth century. Finland's neutrality was officially acknowledged by the Soviet Union in October of 1989. For none of them, however, can neutrality survive in wartime unless the warfighting states respect the lawful integrity of neutral states.

Law is closely linked to *Legitimacy*. Neutrality must, in the same way as alliance membership, be accepted by others as a legitimate

FIGURE 1.1
The LAR pyramid

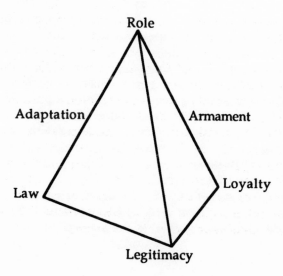

foreign and military policy alternative. The neutrals themselves must make the chosen policy look relevant and credible. Credibility is probably the most difficult aspect of neutrality, because it can be judged against any act, statement, even non-decision, by a neutral government. We will return to this.

In their policies, neutral governments have generally chosen the side of the smaller states. Part of the foreign policies of neutrals includes a special *Loyalty* toward exposed nations or peoples. One aspect of this Loyalty is the demand for a reduction of unequal distribution of wealth and influence and the support of basic human needs and rights. For instance, support of a more equal 'economic world order', much discussed during the 1970s, and solidarity with the problems and difficulties of the developing nations have been repeatedly expressed.

The three L's make up the base of the pyramid. They represent basic attitudes to important global issues. The two A's imply that these attitudes have to be operationalized and implemented. That is a different and more difficult matter than to formulate policy. It is at this stage that the neutral dilemma becomes apparent.

Due to their small size and their international dependencies, the question of *Adaptation* to international transformation becomes crucial. Despite the difficulties involved in defining the meaning and measurement of dependence, it seems an uncontroversial conclusion that developments since 1945 have created increasing latent (potential) dependence of small states upon bigger states and groups of states (see for instance Keohane & Nye 1977; Jones & Willetts 1984; Hagelin 1986; Catrina 1988). Latent dependence is the potential for other governments and organizations to exert pressure upon the smaller states. Part of the dilemma stems from the fact that neutrality implies a certain degree of independence. But to what degree and with regard to what issues?

The answer to that question is at the center of legitimacy. The neutrals must make credible that their policy is an alternative to major-power-dominated policies. They must show that it is possible to retain a certain freedom of action. The general observation has been made that if participation in universal international organizations confers many benefits upon the neutral state while involving very few risks, action within regional organizations may in the long run tarnish the credibility of neutrality (Karsch 1988, p. 62). Such membership might be interpreted, by nations not part of such organizations as 'block orientation'. This, in turn, would imply a reduction of neutral freedom of action and create doubts about the credibility of neutral independence.

Moreover, the more specific the interpretations of the three L's, the less the political freedom in implementing them. Although membership in military alliances is, by definition, impossible for a non-aligned nation, membership in economic organizations is another matter. Although Sweden joined the Organization for European Economic Cooperation (OEEC) without any reservations (Sweden also participated in the Marshall Plan), Finland refrained from either accepting the Marshall Plan or joining the OEEC. Instead, it joined the Organization for Economic Cooperation and Development (OECD), the successor of the OEEC. Switzerland, when joining the OEEC, clarified that the membership was not to be interpreted as a compromise of its neutrality (Karsch 1988, p. 63). All the neutrals have, however, joined the European Free Trade Association (EFTA).

It seems that the less military the issue, and the less controversial with regard to national sovereignty and independence, the easier it has been for the neutrals to adapt to international changes by becoming members of international organizations or to formally cooperate in other forms. Participation in international as well as regional organizations in support of civilian research and development (R&D) or civilian industrial projects, for instance, has generally posed no insurmountable difficulties.

The European Community (EC), however, has been a more complicated matter. Whereas OEEC/OECD and EFTA were perceived of and presented as purely economic frameworks without political constraints, the EC is different. It aims not only at a regional community with a common economic policy and trade barriers toward non-members. It has also developed into a community with political and security, including military-industrial, facets (Sjöstedt 1977).

As a reflection of the dilemma between neutrality and the need for adaptation, it should be noted that although Ireland, another neutral state, is a member of the EC, Finland and Sweden have not accepted membership under the present circumstances. Instead, the EFTA countries are seeking a collective arrangement with the EC. The Swedish rejection of individual and formal membership was made clear in a statement by the then Foreign Minister on April 9, 1972, in connection with the signing of a trade agreement between Sweden and the EC (*Documents on Swedish Foreign Policy* 1972, p. 255). That statement repeated the basic arguments that had been presented by the Swedish Prime Minister in August of 1961 (*Documents on Swedish Foreign Policy* 1961, p. 119). Likewise, in October of 1988 the Finnish government presented a report to Parliament stating that close cooperation, but not membership, was possible and desirable (referred to in *Upsala Nya Tidning*, November 2, 1988).

Contrary to Sweden and Finland, the Austrian government applied for membership in the EC in July of 1989. The application included a demand for remaining neutral. The application has not only created a controversy among the EC members. The Soviet Union, one of the signatory powers of the Austrian State Treaty in 1955, stated in August of 1989 that Austrian membership in the EC would automatically cancel any possibility of Austria realizing its neutral policy. Whether this was a serious Soviet 'threat' or just an attempt to support the critics within the EC is difficult to say. In any event, to accept or to reject Austrian membership will clearly not be an easy decision for the EC to make. It will be a test case for other neutrals who regard membership as a future possibility.

The EC has sharpened the neutral dilemma between economic necessity and political desirability. The economic risk of 'going it alone' is considered high among industrial circles. To put the dilemma in extreme terms, when the EC countries complete the common market in 1992, other nations may have to chose between accepting isolation or seeking integration. Whether neutrals decide to 'go it alone' or to become members of international organizations, the dilemma remains. 'Isolated independence' may be no better than 'integrated dependence'.

In general, the dilemma involved in adaptation can be phrased thus: how to behave in a changing world without risking the legitimacy of neutrality. *Armament*, the second A, poses that question specifically with regard to military policy. There are at least two contradictory attitudes toward the relationship between neutrality and armament. The first is that a neutral nation does not have, and does not need, a military defense. This attitude shows a lack of understanding of the more or less implicit demands upon a neutral state in international law and the existence of domestic interests in favor of armament in peacetime. One might even argue that the basic rational for the present indigenous military production in the neutral countries is not neutrality but the preservation of that industry itself.

The other attitude reflects a more academic approach, namely, whether a neutral country allocates more or less to defense than does a military alliance member. This approach does not build upon the first notion that neutrality as such implies no military defense. The Stockholm International Peace Research Institute (SIPRI) has concluded that the question is impossible to answer (*World Armaments and Disarmament* 1987, p. 135). Attempts have nevertheless been made to develop a method to solve this controversial issue (see Murdoch & Sandler 1986).

Adaptation and *Armament* combined pose one of the most serious dilemmas with regard to neutral policy. All of the four neutral countries studied here have accepted a policy of 'armed neutrality' supported by some indigenous military production. At the same time, they support international and regional arms control and disarmament. The neutral governments also have restrictive foreign military sales policies – military sales are to be regarded as exceptions rather than as the rule. But due to increasing costs and technological demands, a restrictive military sales policy complicates the ambition to support advanced indigenous military production. Foreign military sales may therefore become an increasingly important ingredient in sustaining 'armed neutrality' by indigenous means.

There are, in other words, serious political difficulties in combining the basic attitudes expressed by the three L's with the ambitions and difficulties involved in the two A's. If the gap becomes too wide, the *Role* of neutrality may be at stake. The Swedish Prime Minister has acknowledged that pursuing an active policy for international disarmament and non-military solutions to conflict has become more complicated since Swedish arms have shown up in unacceptable recipient countries (*Anförande* 1988, p. 12). With reference to figure 1.1, in order to avoid some obvious dilemmas, the neutral *Role* must be defined as the logical extention of, and must be in harmony with, the basic attitudes and their realization. This harmonization involves both the formal and the actual policy.

Foreign military sales have therefore become an important issue in the policy of neutrality itself. The problems involved in foreign military sales relate to several general issues of importance to the role and standing of neutrality in the global society.

1.2   FOREIGN MILITARY SALES

This study is about Austria, Finland, Sweden and Switzerland. These non-aligned states have accepted a policy of 'armed neutrality'. This means a policy supported not only by military force but by certain indigenous military production. Domestic military research and development (R&D) as well as manufacture have been defined as important for the credibility of an independent and armed non-aligned policy in peace-time and successful neutrality in wartime.

But the economic and technological conditions for armed neutrality have changed since 1945. Inflation, personnel costs and the cost of new technology have increased the financial pressure upon sustaining a military establishment in general and military production in particular. Military materiel has become more expensive (Olsson 1977; Hagelin 1985). Government orders for indigenously developed military

8 *Introduction*

materiel have therefore become less frequent and less automatic. The result is a dilemma for the neutral governments in adapting to changing economic and technological circumstances on the one hand, and armament as a national policy, on the other. This dilemma is the result of the push and pull between what is perceived as economic necessity and political desirability. George Thayer in 1970 remarked about the 'ironies of the arms trade' that Sweden and Switzerland, both neutrals with long histories of peace, were then among the world's most agressive suppliers (Thayer 1970, p. 21). In 1978 Anthony Sampson noted with particular reference to Sweden that pressures would increase further on the dilemma of combining armed neutrality with commercial viability as the cost of self-sufficiency became heavier (Sampson 1978, pp. 298-299).

The reactions by the neutral governments have been to find ways to support indigenous military production despite diminishing domestic orders. Three main solutions have been tried. First, countries have instigated national rationalizations through industrial mergers and specialization. For the non-aligned countries there is one basic difficulty with this option, namely, that they already have a relatively small number of major military producers. Savings may nevertheless be possible in some categories of materiel, such as the production of ammunition. In Sweden and Finland the production of ships may also be further rationalized, as may guided missile production in Sweden.

Second, attempts have been made by some military producers to increase civilian production. There are several difficulties with this alternative. Many military producers have only limited knowledge of the civilian market. They are accustomed to one major and easily recognized buyer, their own government. Competition has also been limited because national military markets are protected.

Success in civilian markets demands risky investments in a market in which the buyer is not easily recognized. Marketing demands new knowledge as well as capital. But most of all, success demands competitive civilian products which more often than not require less technological sophistication than those demanded by the military. The military market has therefore not only been a protected market. It has also created a technological 'over-skill' on the part of the producers, a technological sophistication which is not directly suited to or necessary for civilian demands. Also, neither the neutral governments nor the industries themselves have so far been willing to allocate the capital needed for large-scale civilian trials and errors.

Thus, as long as national military production is politically accepted and supported, military producers have a tendency to stick to their traditional military products and compete with well-known means. Successful conversion to civilian production more often than not constitutes a spin-off from, rather than an alternative to, military production. The demands for follow-up military contracts by the traditional military producers have in most cases remained high. The main result of increased civilian production has therefore been diversification rather than conversion.

Third, foreign military sales, in combination with different forms of international exchange of goods, services and know-how, have become a most important complement to a reduced domestic military market. John Stanley and Maurice Pearton in 1972 reached what they considered the 'ironic conclusion' that (Stanley & Pearton 1972, p. 67) 'the expense of modern weapons development makes it impossible for a neutral nation to arm itself at a politically acceptable cost without substantial export sales which themselves must eventually compromise neutrality'.

A non-aligned policy means not only staying out of military alliances but also staying impartial in international conflicts. One difficulty with foreign military sales is that over time they increase the possibility of the producing nation becoming involved as a military supplier to one or more participants in an armed conflict. This possibility can be assumed to increase, first, if the number of recipients increases, and, second, if sales are accepted to politically unstable regions or countries. The reason is that weapons and other military materiel are bought with the aim not only to deter but also to be used.

Even if direct involvement in a military conflict does not occur, foreign military sales fuel the global arms market and the militarization of conflict – two developments which the non-aligned governments say they wish to see controlled and reduced. This is bad enough because the issue of a credible non-aligned policy can be understood in terms of *expectations*. In a world which to a large extent is defined by major power rivalry, military alliances, armed conflicts and regional as well as a global arms race, a non-aligned foreign policy could be expected to aim for and support a different world.

One expected ingredient in such a different world is a restrictive foreign military sales policy. Military sales should either not be permitted at all or should be defined and controlled by restrictive foreign military sales control requirements. But at the same time, a restrictive military sales policy could complicate the ambition to support indigenous military production and reduce the margins of profit for the producers. This may be one piece of the puzzle explaining the existence of illegal military sales.

The number of disclosed or alleged illegal foreign military sales cases involving industries or individuals from neutral countries are by now numerous. For instance, the European Association for the Study of Safety Problems in the Production of Propellant Powder, in reality an international powder cartel, was uncovered by the Swedish customs authorities during the 1980s. The cartel was established in 1975 and included companies in several Western European countries including Sweden (Nobel Kemi), Finland (Forcit and Kemira), and Switzerland (Wimmis and Societé Suisse Explosifs). It is said to have been dissolved in 1986. Among its customers was Iran before and during the war with Iraq. SIPRI concluded in 1986 (*World Armaments and Disarmament* 1986, p. 334): 'Big companies often seem to lack the local expertise enjoyed by small trading companies and they are sometimes reluctant to be connected with deals in countries such as Iran'.

Forcit is known to have cooperated with Swedish companies in order to hide the final destination of some of its powder. If the Finnish powder was defined as an ingredient in upgraded Swedish powder, the transaction would not have to be defined as a re-transfer when the powder was finally exported from Sweden. In November of 1989 it was clear, however, that a number of individuals at Forcit will be put to trial for illegal exports. The incident was, moreover, one reason for the inclusion of 'end-manufacturing certificates' in Swedish control requirements (see Chapter 4).

Financial 'clearinghouses' for transferring and hiding funds are a crucial part of illegal sales. Switzerland has perhaps the world's best system for performing such services. Anthony Sampson concluded in 1978 that Switzerland had become the 'indispensable haven for arms dealers everywhere, from Lockheed and Northrop to shady suppliers and hijackers' (Sampson 1978, p. 298).

Recently, Switzerland was mentioned not only in connection with illegal sales from Sweden but with the Iran-contra investigation in the United States (*Iran-Contra Affair* 1987, p. 332). Information suggests that all of the four neutrals studied here have supplied military supplies to the Iran-Iraq war with or without the knowledge or consent of their respective governments. At least three of them have supplied military supplies to both parties (*World Armaments and Disarmament* 1987, pp. 204-205).

While the year of 1968 for many individuals is forever remembered by student uprisings and the Soviet invasion of Czechoslovakia, it is in Switzerland also remembered by 'the Bührle scandal'. In November of that year it was revealed that Oerlikon-Bührle had illegally exported arms to Nigeria and other countries with the use of false end-use certificates. One sales director, one deputy director and one managing clerk were arrested and sentenced by court decision (Sampson 1978, p. 298; *World Armaments and Disarmament* 1968/69, pp. 87-88).

In Austria illegal sales were also brought to light at a relatively early date. During the 1970s, a scandal concerning Syria led to the resignation of the then Austrian Minister of Defense (*Dagens Nyheter*, June 1, 1977). Again in 1985 criminal investigations began into the sale of Austrian guns and ammunition by the Voest-Alpine subsidiary Noricum to both Iran and Iraq. Even though these allegations were rejected by the Ministry for Industry, a former member of Noricum publicly acknowledged in early 1988 that the company had sold weapons to Iran via Libya (*Svenska Dagbladet*, September 17, 1987; *Upsala Nya Tidning*, January 27, 1988). The President of Noricum was prosecuted for selling howitzers to Iran and for having offered that country an artillery factory (*World Armaments and Disarmament* 1988, p. 194). In late September of 1989 the Austrian Parliament decided to make an investigation of the illegal sales to Iran.

These examples illustrate that all of the neutrals have been noted for illegal or alleged illegal sales. This study will not, however, delve further into illegal or 'gray area' military sales. Instead, it will attempt to analyze and explain the role of foreign military sales in the armament policies of the neutrals, that is military sales as legitimate policy. What constitutes a restrictive foreign military sales policy? Do the neutrals reflect such a policy and if so to what extent? How critical is the dilemma described here, and how have the neutral governments tried to solve it? How can similarities and differences in non-aligned foreign military sales policies be explained? What are the prospects for a 'directed' neutral alternative in military sales? These are questions that this study addresses and attempts to answer.

1.3 PREVIOUS STUDIES

Studies of relevance to the issue of neutral foreign military sales policy can be divided into three categories: studies of why and how nations arm, studies of foreign military sales, and specific studies of the non-aligned nations. Attempts to explain why and how nations arm are found in two major theoretical schools. The first tries to explain armaments mainly as a result of international factors. The second sees domestic factors as the main determinants. The first school includes geopolitical studies and the 'realistic' approach within political science. Lewis F. Richardson's mathematical study in 1960 can be considered the starting point for the most influential theoretical approach within this group, namely the action-reaction theories (Richardson 1960).

Action-reaction theories generally focus upon pairs of antagonistic major powers. Nations are treated as unified and rational actors. The oversimplifications in this mainly quantitative theoretical approach lead to the reaction of the second school. Alternative theories formulated during the 1970s took as their starting-point more or less self-generating forces within the nations themselves. These theories do not confine themselves to antagonistic powers or bilateral 'arms races'. Instead these theories include more varied explanatory factors such as bureaucratic processes, conflicting interests among groups and individuals, pressure groups, as well as economic and technological constraints and demands (see, for instance, Halperin 1974; Greenwood 1975). The so called military-industrial complex theory is the core approach of this group (Senghaas 1972; Melman 1974; Rosen 1975), which may also include studies of major international arms contracts (Boulton 1978; Dörfer 1983). Although studies of major powers prevail, this approach includes more studies of smaller nations than does the first school of theories (see Zinnes et al. 1976; Cooling 1981; Mintz 1985).

Neither of the two schools can, on its own, fully explain armament acquisitions and dynamics. The different theoretical approaches have therefore been combined and further developed. In particular, the general impact of science and technology has been noted. One example, formulated during the 1960s from personal experience, is the Kranzberg theory of the 'push and pull' among science, technology and military use (Kranzberg 1969). According to Kranzberg there is no linear or directly causal relationship which links a scientific discovery, its development and its application as a useful product. Instead, there is constant feedback between civilian and military sciences and among research, development and application. The more recent 'technological front' explanation formulated by the Swedish historian Wilhelm Agrell also focuses upon the close relationships between civilian and military science and technology (Agrell 1981, 1989).

Foreign military sales cannot take place without the production of military supplies. Thus, the second category of studies, those of foreign military sales, should be a logical extension of studies about why and how nations arm. As noted by Stephanie Neuman and Robert Harkavy in 1980, it is neither possible nor wise to attempt to isolate foreign military sales from their surrounding context (Neuman & Harkavy 1980, p. 315). But this is exactly what has often been done, especially in the early literature. The question of how and why nations arm has been treated as relevant foremost to nations performing indigenous military R&D. Studies of foreign military sales, however, have focused to a large extent upon the recipients, especially countries which lack military R&D facilities.

The first studies of foreign military sales were essentially data compilations. In 1966, SIPRI took the lead in focusing upon the sale of major weapons to the Third World (*World Armaments and Disarmament* 1969; *The Arms Trade with the Third World* 1971; Brzoska & Ohlson 1987). Not until the 1970s did SIPRI broaden its focus to include industrial recipients and non-major weapons. Other institutes publishing similar annual compilations are the Arms Control and Disarmament Agency (ACDA) in Washington, D.C. (*World Military Expenditures and Arms Transfers*), and the International Institute for Strategic Studies (IISS) in London (*Strategic Survey*). The SIPRI, ACDA and IISS publications are standard references in studies of foreign military sales.

David Louscher and Michael Salomone have divided the literature on military sales into three groups: descriptions of trends and modes of transfer, discussions about the consequences, and policy recommendations about what to do (Louscher & Salomone 1987, pp. 24-25). Most studies are descriptive and fall into the first two groups. The third group is made up of the arms control and disarmament literature in which studies of what has become known as 'alternative' or 'defensive' military postures should also be included (see *Journal of Peace Research* 1984).

In the group of descriptive studies, most deal with major suppliers. Several also aim at supporting a particular view, for instance, that foreign sales are a necessary part of a nation's foreign policy (see Moodie 1979; Pierre 1979; Sorley 1983; Neuman 1986). Among smaller suppliers, Israel can also be included in this category (Klieman 1985). In a recent study, William Bajusz and David Louscher (Bajusz & Louscher 1988) attempted to quantify the impact upon the United States of restricted foreign military sales to the Middle East in particular. Bajusz and Louscher argued for continued American military sales.

Louscher and Salomone did not mention theoretical studies as a separate group. This omission seems to be a correct reflection of reality. Although several authors claim to use a theoretical approach, well-formulated and ready-to-be-tested theories are few. Therefore, it is not possible to distinguish among anything resembling well-defined theoretical 'schools' of foreign military sales. Neuman and Harkavy, in their 1980 study, tried to integrate different insights concerning military trade. Nevertheless, their book reflected the traditional tendency to focus upon major Western suppliers and Third World recipients despite attempts by some contributors to introduce new theoretical ideas (such as Kolodziej 1980). The editors even concluded that (Neuman & Harkavy 1980, p. 315) 'the subject is quite probably of a complexity well beyond the level where one might contemplate tight casual models, and explicitly set forth formal relationships between sets of dependent and independent variables'.

This conclusion is probably too pessimistic. Foreign military sales still constitute a relatively young area in terms of academic research. Although non-aligned nations, most often Sweden and Switzerland, have been included in general and descriptive works (Thayer 1970; Stanley & Pearton 1972; Sampson 1978), it is only recently that analytical monographs have been published about the individual foreign military sales policies of the non-aligned nations (*Waffenplatz Schweiz* 1983; Huru et al. 1984; Hagelin 1985; Andersson & Stenquist 1988; Westander 1988).

Comparative studies, particularly involving smaller nations, are especially rare. Neuman and Harkavy identified this as a particular area for future investigation. Another future research area that they mentioned is the impact of public opinion upon foreign military sales. This book is an attempt to fill part of this void by comparing the foreign military sales policies of the four European non-aligned countries using public opinion as one explanatory factor. The theoretical approach developed in Chapter 2 is called the REstrictive FOReign MIlitary Sales (REFORMIS) approach.

1.4   ABOUT THE STATISTICAL SOURCES

One particular difficulty in studies about almost any area of military affairs is the availability and validity of information. Despite the general openness of the societies under study, militarily related information can still be difficult to find. Sweden and Austria illustrate two quite different situations with regard to the access of foreign military sales information. In Austria detailed information on military sales is scarce (Pilz 1982; van der Bellen et al. 1985), and there are no regular official reports about Austrian foreign military sales. In Sweden there has been an increase in information about military sales especially since 1983. In that year a law concerning foreign military sales was passed, including provisions for more public information. Each year since 1984 the Swedish government has presented information about war materiel sales during the preceding year to the Swedish Parliament (*Regeringens skrivelse* 1984).

Figures showing Swedish war materiel sales are of two kinds. One kind is the foreign trade statistics published by the National Central

Bureau of Statistics (SCB). These statistics are generated from information supplied by the customs authorities. The other is an annual compilation by the War Materiel Inspectorate (KMI), which is part of the trade division within the Ministry for Foreign Affairs. These latter compilations are identical to the government presentations to the Parliament and are based upon information supplied by the producing and exporting companies. Because all categories of war materiel cannot be extracted from the SCB figures, this book relies upon KMI data.

No compilations similar to the Swedish KMI statistics are available in Switzerland or Finland. The figures used here for those countries are based upon figures from their respective national customs authorities. They were compiled by the authors of the various national studies (Hug 1987; Joenniemi 1987; Pilz 1987). In order to analyze the comparability of KMI and customs authority figures, Swedish KMI figures were first compared with distinguishable and relevant categories of war materiel from the SCB foreign trade statistics for the years 1970-1985. The comparison (not published) showed that although figures for individual categories of war materiel sometimes varied considerably between the two Swedish sources, the annual aggregates did not. Second, the goods defined as war materiel and included in national statistics are almost identical in the countries studied here. Therefore, comparisons of neutral foreign military sales seem possible as long as they do not involve detailed comparisons of categories of war materiel.

It has been particularly difficult to check the validity of the military sales figures. This problem will be discussed more in the text wherever appropriate. Here it should only be noted that this is a problem that has been further emphasized by illegal sales from the neutral countries. The value of illegal sales is either totally excluded from the official statistics, or it is included in the value of sales to a legitimate recipient which is not, however, the final user. Instead, the supplies are re-transferred to the so called end user. The value of this illegal re-transfer is, in such cases, not separately visible in the statistics.

A former Bofors director has stated that the manipulation of export statistics caused by the re-transfer of war materiel is hardly of relevance to the neutral countries because they are all legitimate recipients (*Svenska Dagbladet*, December 10, 1988, p. 6). His point may be true as long as the end user is that same neutral country. But if not, his statements can imply just the opposite: Because they are legitimate recipients, the non-aligned nations may be used in deliberate attempts by the supplier to re-transfer war materiel to unauthorized end users.

Without more information about illegal re-transfers, it is impossible to make adjustments for such sales. Illegal sales are not included here mainly for two reasons. First, new information continues to come out – particularly in Sweden – which makes it difficult to sketch a reasonably distinct picture even of what has happened so far. Second, until all the facts and preferably all the original documents are made available to the public, information will remain unreliable and incomplete. Because it is highly unlikely that all the facts or documents will ever be made public – or, for that matter, that documents that can undo these difficulties exist at all – much of the uncertainty surrounding illegal sales is probably lasting.

This does not mean that all information about illegal sales is totally irrelevant for the understanding of foreign military sales in general. For a comparative study such as this one, however, a particular difficulty is that information is very uneven. Even though it is possible to estimate how much of Swedish sales to Great Britain (by FFV) and to Singapore (by Bofors) were re-transferred, it is much more difficult to make such estimates for the other neutrals. Moreover, although many known illegal sales have been of relatively low value, the total magnitude of the illegal market is unknown. For these reasons, it is assumed here that the value of illegal sales via the neutrals is negligible.

Much of the specific information used in this book is taken from the national case studies prepared for the common project and from discussions with the group members. In their studies, the individual authors have mainly used available national information. Military information is in many cases difficult to obtain. This explains why some of the figures have not been updated. Moreover, information which is available in one country is not always available or completely comparable to such information published in another country. A major effort has been made to reduce such inconsistencies. These difficulties are also further discussed in the text.

1.5   KEY CONCEPTS

A few terms used throughout this study are important to understand before we continue. *Military production* is used as a general term referring to the process by which military supplies are created and acquired. The process includes research, development, manufacture and delivery. These steps do not necessarily occur in a logical sequence. For

TABLE 1.1
Official definitions of war materiel: content of military supplies as defined, national statistical coverage and domestic production of supplies*

Materiel Categories	Austria C	Austria S	Austria P	Finland C	Finland S	Finland P	Sweden C	Sweden S	Sweden P	Switzerland C	Switzerland S	Switzerland P
Aircraft												
• light	x					x			x			
• fighters	x			x	x		x	x		x	x	x
Guided missiles				x	x		x	x	x	x	x	x
Ships												
• light						x			x			
• warships						x			x			x
Armored vehicles	x		x	x	x	x	x	x	x	x	x	x
Artillery	x		x	x	x	x	x	x	x	x	x	x
Light arms	x		x	x	x	x	x	x	x	x	x	x
Explosives and munition	x		x	x	x	x	x	x	x	x	x	x
Spare parts	x		x	x	x	x	x	x	x	x	x	x

* C = covered by definition of war materiel; S = statistical coverage; P = production.

instance, manufacture can be in the form of license manufacture without previous indigenous R&D. Neither does delivery only mean delivery to one's own national military establishment; the term can also refer to foreign military sales.

Military supplies is a collective term for goods (materiel), know-how and services. Only *conventional* supplies are studied here; atomic/nuclear, biological and chemical military supplies are excluded. *Important military materiel* refers to major conventional weapons – aircraft, armored vehicles, ships and guided missiles. These goods are central to the main tasks of the three military services (the Air Force, the Army, and the Navy).

The term *foreign military sales* is used instead of 'arms sales' or 'arms trade' because the term *arms* mainly connotes weapons. 'Military' is a more general term which includes other military supplies. With regard to sales by the neutrals, the term *military* is also more appropriate because a large portion of neutral foreign military sales is made up of powder and ammunition.

Although foreign military sales is an 'outward' activity (export), the term *military trade* also includes the 'inward' activity of import. In addition, the term encompasses the new modes of sale which have evolved during the last twenty years in the global market such as barter, offsets and other types of international cooperation for the production and exchange of military supplies.

When referring specifically to military production and sales as officially defined by the neutral governments, the term *war materiel* is used. There are two aspects of this term that are important to keep in mind. First, it generally refers only to goods 'specifically designed for military use', not to other military supplies. The only exception is found in Sweden, where manufacturing licenses (a type of know-how) are included in the control requirements. Swedish statistics do not, however, include the value of such licenses.

Second, war materiel is covered by national foreign military sales statistics. Because only officially accepted military sales are analyzed in this book, the official statistics used throughout the study refer to war materiel. Whenever other statistical sources are used, the differences and consequences are described.

Table 1.1 shows that most war materiel is identically covered by national statistical sources in three of the four countries. Normally, when military supplies are indigenously produced and defined as war materiel, they are also covered by statistical sources. Switzerland has no Navy; thus warship production is irrelevant for Switzerland. The production of ships in Austria refers to the manufacture of light patrol boats for use on the Danube.

In Austria, Finland and Switzerland certain war materiel that is not indigenously produced is included in the control framework, such as fighter aircraft and/or missiles. In Austria no aircraft is produced. The major difference between Austria and the others, however, is that no official Austrian foreign military sales statistics are published.

1.6 ABOUT THIS STUDY

The main theoretical tool, the REFORMIS approach, is developed in Chapter 2. The approach distinguishes between *formal* foreign military sales *policy* and *actual* foreign military *sales*. In section 2.1 a restrictive foreign military sales policy is defined. The REFORMIS approach suggests how such a restrictive policy comes about in the form of control requirements (section 2.2). In section 2.3 different foreign military sales outcomes are defined depending upon the implementation of formal policy. The expected outcome for each of the neutrals is postulated.

In order to understand some basic factors that have shaped the military production in Austria, Finland, Sweden and Switzerland after 1945, Chapter 3 describes and compares their modern military history as well as certain military industry indicators. Just as it is difficult to estimate the value of illegal sales from the neutrals, it is difficult to estimate legal sales from foreign-based subsidiaries of military producers in the neutral nations. Such sales are not controlled in any of the neutrals and are therefore not visible in the statistics. In order to estimate the importance of such indirect modes of sale, Chapter 3 includes a discussion of what is known about different modes of neutral foreign military sales and their most likely importance for the quantitative indicators used.

The main findings with regard to foreign military sales are presented in Chapter 4. The control requirements are compared in section 4.1. In section 4.2 actual foreign military sales are analyzed and compared with the postulated outcomes, focusing upon the period from 1970 to 1987. A special question in this book is whether a directed neutral foreign military sales alternative is realistic. Section 4.2 therefore also includes information about foreign military sales among the neutrals. In Chapter 5 the neutrals are studied from the point of view of global military cooperation or competition.

In Chapter 6 the main conclusions are summarized. In the final analysis, section 6.2, four different neutral alternatives are discussed. They exemplify different stages of neutral coordination and co-operation. Three of them are armament alternatives based upon a continued policy of armed neutrality. The fourth alternative is based upon a different neutral role.

2

The REFORMIS Approach:
A Framework for Understanding
Neutral Foreign Military Sales
Policy

2.1   A RESTRICTIVE MILITARY SALES POLICY

All the neutrals have restrictions on their foreign military sales. Two
sets of restrictions – unconditional and conditional – are included in the
formal policy. Unconditional restrictions exist in all of the four countries. They are the result of international agreements such as the
Hague Conventions or membership in international organizations such
as the United Nations. Although not a member of the United Nations,
Switzerland has participated in international arms embargoes recom-
mended or decided by the U.N. Security Council.

Unconditional restrictions are normally limited in time and are
relevant only to a few and very particular recipients. Most neutral
foreign military sales fall, therefore, under unilateral and conditional
control requirements. In principle, formal military sales policies can be
restrictive or permissive. At the extremes, one finds either a total and
unconditional embargo policy or a totally free and uncontrolled military sales policy. Because all the neutrals maintain military production supported by foreign military sales while they at the same
time impose foreign military sales restrictions, none of them belongs to
either of these two extremes. Instead, neutral policy reflects degrees of
restrictiveness.

A decision to accept or to reject a foreign military sales application is made on a case-by-case basis by the government or a representative of the government. The decision is normally made under the auspices of the Ministry of Foreign Affairs, Defense, or Industry. When accepted, an export permit is issued to the relevant military producer and supplier. In order to understand the nature of neutral foreign military sales and the restrictiveness of policy, we need to look at the individual control requirements in detail.

There are several possible ways of interpreting a restrictive policy, for instance,

by way of control requirements:
• Number of requirements and/or
• their coverage;
by the implementation of the control requirements:
• In a strict or
• in a loose way;
by the balance between rejected and accepted foreign military sales applications:
• In terms of the frequency of accepted applications and/or
• with regard to the percentage of accepted applications;
by the size of the foreign military market:
• The number and type of recipients and/or
• the value of foreign military sales in total or by recipient;
by legal action:
• In terms of the government's response in general to alleged illegal foreign military sales and/or
• by the preparedness to accept punitive action.

The first interpretation of a restrictive policy is central to the approach developed here. The number of individual control requirements and their coverage define the relative restrictiveness of the policy – the more control requirements and the broader their coverage, the more restrictive the formal policy. This is further developed in section 2.2.

A restrictive formal policy ought to be reflected in actual foreign military sales. This policy is achieved by a strict implementation of the control requirements. If not, actual military sales may even contradict formal policy. The implementation of formal policy is therefore very important and is discussed in section 2.3.

The government can handle the military export applications from industry in different ways. During a period of time, it can accept only a certain frequency or percentage of all foreign military sales applications. If the frequency or share is low, the policy can be defined as restrictive. As will be discussed, however, part of formal policy is not public. Even if the total number of applications is public knowledge, a decision to accept or to reject a foreign military sale application is normally not. This interpretation is therefore not further developed here.

Quantifications of foreign military sales are generally made in terms of the number of recipients and the value of sales. Such quantitative indicators are important in the REFORMIS approach because they are measures of actual foreign military sales. Their theoretical importance is discussed in section 2.3. The actual foreign military sales are analyzed in Chapters 4 and 5.

Attempts to define a restrictive formal policy by way of legal action applies only to illegal sales. Because illegal sales are not included in this book, this definition is left out of the approach developed here. Nevertheless, as was indicated in Chapter 1, illegal sales may also be understood in terms of the REFORMIS approach.

To summarize: In defining and analyzing the foreign military sales policies of the neutrals, two sets of indicators will be used:

- national control requirements (defining formal policy) and
- (actual) foreign military sales indicators, reflecting the political implementation of the control requirements.

2.2 FORMAL POLICY

The neutral dilemma with regard to foreign military sales has two important dimensions. The first is a national political dimension, namely, that a restrictive foreign military sales policy complicates the ambition to support indigenous military production by way of foreign sales. The second is a closely related international dimension: Changes in the global military market affect the conditions for solving the national dimension of the dilemma. Over time, more suppliers have been introduced on the international market. Since 1945, foreign military sales have changed from dealing with surplus goods to modern materiel; from gifts or politically motivated price reductions to commercial sales for profit; from the sale of finished goods to 'package' contracts including materiel as well as services (such as training) and know-how (through technology transfers and manufacturing rights). To make such 'package deals' possible, payment has become a form of 'barter' and offset; instead of (only) paying in cash, payment can be in the form of two-way exchange and/or international industrial cooperation (see *World Armaments and Disarmament* 1984, 1985; Ohlson 1988).

In order to participate in international military competition, it has become necessary to adapt to (accept) recipient demands. It is proposed here that a restrictive formal foreign military sales policy has become increasingly difficult to realize for the following reasons:

* the domestic military market is increasingly unable to support indigenous military production because military production is becoming more expensive and because military demands have to compete with other pressing social demands upon the main buyer, the government;
* to maintain indigenous military production, foreign military sales have become a *direct necessity* for, rather than an *indirect effect of*, such production;
* the international market is increasingly being shaped by long-term cooperative agreements rather than by competition for limited, one-time and one-way sales. The forms of competition have changed due to the technological complexity and capital requirements of advanced military production.

These tendencies affect the formulation of policy with respect to military sales. The economic imperatives involved in military sales direct policy so as to support flexibility in regulations and implementation (freedom of action). Neutrality concerns, however, direct policy so as to reduce the effects of increased military sales that compromise the credibility and legitimization of the neutral policy. Foreign military sales policy is formulated in a push and pull between these two directions.

Two important conditions work in support of military production and sales: the direct and often discrete contacts among industry representatives, the military leadership and the government, on the one hand, and the secret aspects of foreign military sales policy, on the other. It should be remembered that armed neutrality is 'established' policy. There exists, therefore, a common interest in armed neutrality among influential policy individuals, agencies and groups, on the one hand, and the military-industrial leadership (and employees), on the other. The military leadership can be assumed to support indigenous military production as long as the end product is internationally competitive.

This is not to say that there is a conspiracy, as was often implied in the early military-industrial complex theories. Rather, the common interest can be defined as a 'military-industrial-political brotherhood'. Although the term was coined with particular reference to Sweden (Hagelin 1983), this brotherhood can also be assumed to exist in the other neutrals. The result is a commonly anticipated need for sustained indigenous military production, which in order to be affordable must include foreign military sales as well as other modes of military trade.

As a result, when a government or government agency decides in favor of a particular military sale, the importance of individual control requirements may be reduced in favor of economic and other perceived benefits from foreign military sales. Although such benefits are seldom, if ever, explicitly referred to – this belongs to the secret part of policy – several arguments have been formulated in general support of foreign military sales. They include continuous employment and technological benefits for the producers; lower acquisition costs for the government by way of longer production runs, which reduce the price per item; sustained preparedness of production in case of a possible future conflict; and balance-of-trade benefits for the nation. A particular small-state argument is the assumed benefit for the recipient of avoiding political strings from a major supplier (see Hagelin 1985, 1988).

Because the important support of military production and foreign military sales come from the military-industrial-political brotherhood, where would critique against foreign military sales come from? Even if there exist individuals within the brotherhood who are opposed to foreign military sales in general – or, more likely, to individual deals or recipients – they can be assumed to be few and/or to have difficulties in making their voices heard. Very few are willing to risk their employment; instead, they are likely to keep inopportune views to themselves.

Critique can therefore be assumed to come mainly from individuals and institutions not connected with the brotherhood. Because armed neutrality is traditional official policy, criticism has to be broad and/or has to address a particular issue that cannot be swept aside by the government as illegitimate. This is achieved when foreign military sales become a public issue. Neutrality creates expectations of a restrictive foreign military sales policy. This does not mean, however, that this policy is constantly debated. An aware, concerned and active public opinion is needed for debate to occur. Public awareness and concern are stimulated through national and international media and through information from informed groups and individuals. The 'trigger' may be the presentation of formerly unknown information, a particular deal that seems to contradict neutral policy,

or illegal sales. Public debate and demands for new control requirements are the visible effects of public awareness and concern.

The government functions as the arbitrator. It is caught between
demands from the military-industrial-political brotherhood for a
more permissive military sales policy and the public's demand for
increasing restrictions. Even though they may want to, policymakers
cannot be totally insensitive to public opinion. The neutral countries
are all democracies, and the politicians are elected by the public. A
restrictive formal policy is therefore a compromise that will have
broad political and public support. Once the public has become aware,
violations – real or perceived – of formal policy will stimulate further
concern over military sales. Such violations will lead to new demands
for even more rigorous controls. Thus, once the neutral dilemma has
been recognized by a broad and recognizable part of the public,
demands for more foreign military sales will clash with interests
which demand more restrictions.

The government is here included in the brotherhood and is thus
assumed to support indigenous military production. A preferable alternative for the government may therefore be to do as little as possible to
complicate foreign military sales. Public demands for increasing
controls clearly complicate the government's position. It may therefore
try to reduce or at least retard public awareness and concern by
exercising secrecy and limiting information about foreign military
sales. Through such a policy the government may hope to keep the
issue off the political agenda.

In Austria no statistical information about war materiel sales is
available to the public. Although such a total rejection of public
information does not exist in the other neutrals, there is a hidden part
of their foreign military sales policy as well. In none of the neutrals,
for instance, are foreign military sales decisions disclosed. Secrecy is
accepted by the political system as long as it is assumed, first, to be
necessary, and, second, that foreign military sales decisions are implemented in accordance with formal policy. This acceptance is based
upon political confidence and trust between the government and the
public through elected members of Parliament.

The REFORMIS approach suggests that as long as foreign military
sales are not recognized by the public as an important issue – that is, as
long as the public is not aware of or concerned about the dilemma
involved in foreign military sales – government decisions can be
expected to be made according to previous practice and more or less
routine procedure. Such decisions can be assumed to be in support of
military production and, if necessary, foreign military sales. Public

demands are necessary in order to make foreign military sales policy more restrictive.

Formal foreign military sales policy is here defined as the combined result of the number of control requirements and their coverage. The government's solution to the conflict of interest between public demands and brotherhood demands create foreign military sales policy. The number and coverage of those requirements reflect in the REFORMIS approach the combined result of public awareness and concern over the foreign military sales issue and the political willingness to accept these demands through changes in the formal military sales policy.

2.3   THE IMPLEMENTATION OF FORMAL POLICY

The importance of the implementation of foreign military sales policy was noted in an official Swedish report in 1987. It concluded (*Försvarsindustrins utlandsverksamhet* 1987, pp. 27-28, author's translation):

> 'There are differences, however, in the implementation, especially with regard to the choice of recipient countries. Several countries pursue export controls which to a large extent are similar to the ones in Sweden. A few countries, however, give permission to export war materiel to considerably more states than is done in Sweden and other countries with roughly the same attitude toward war materiel sales as in Sweden'.

Those 'few countries' were not defined, nor were the recipient countries. The quote is nevertheless important in its admittance that control requirements are insufficient in shaping actual sales. The problems involved in implementing military sales control requirements were further emphasized a year later in another report studying alleged illegal Swedish military sales (*Medborgarkommissionens rapport* 1988, pp. 190-200). To understand foreign military sales policy we must therefore take into account the implementation of formal policy.

Because individual government decisions are secret, they cannot be directly analyzed. Instead, the analysis here is based upon actual foreign military sales. Actual foreign military sales (the outcomes) are the 'shadows' of foreign military sales decisions. In order for the shadows to be visible two necessary conditions have to be present. First, a decision has to be made to accept rather than to reject foreign

military sales to a particular recipient. Second, the relevant supplier
has to be successful in international competition with other suppliers.

Figure 2.1 defines four possible neutral foreign military sales
outcomes: A, B, C and D. The combination of formal policy and the
implementation of the control requirements define the respective
outcomes. They may be named Restraint, Legitimization, Domestic
Policy Tool and Business as Usual, respectively. The four outer corners
of the figure represent four different and extreme policy alternatives:
strong moral policy (upper left), power politics (upper right), double
moral standards (lower left) and 'merchants of death' (lower right).

Where should the line be drawn between a more and a less restrictive formal policy? How many or what type of control requirements should define a more restrictive policy? The answer is difficult
to give and must depend upon the particular nature of the study. As far
as this book is concerned, it will be possible to categorize the neutrals
in relative terms after we have analyzed their formal policy in
detail.

Any restrictive policy requires political control. Such control requires that the government be well informed. The broader the coverage
of control requirements, the more information available to the government. The more information available, the greater the possibilities

FIGURE 2.1
Foreign military sales outcomes

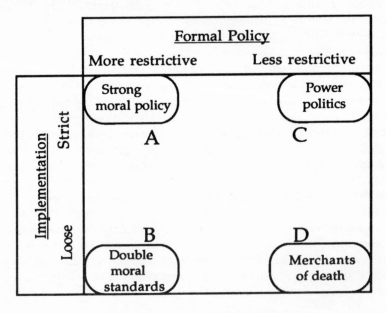

for effective control. These points are worth emphasizing because the term *control* might be intuitively interpreted as identical to a strict implementation of formal policy by the government. This is not necessarily so. It is this distinction which makes it crucial to draw a line between the formal policy and the implementation of policy.

Whether the possibilities for control are used or not depends upon the government's attitude toward foreign military sales in general and toward the control requirements in particular. It is at this stage that the government's role as arbitrator becomes crucial. In order to be restrictive, a foreign military sales policy must not only be formally restrictive. The implementation of the control requirements has also to be strict. In other words, the government should take the control requirements seriously.

Strict implementation of a more restrictive formal policy means that the government is well informed and that the information is taken into account when a decision is being made. In short, the government is 'in control', and the outcome is Restraint. How can this outcome be operationalized?

Let us repeat some important characteristics of being neutral. To be non-aligned means to stand free from military alliances. The foreign policy of a neutral country needs to be different from the foreign policies of the major powers in order to strengthen the credibility of non-alignment in peacetime and of neutrality in wartime. For the neutrals studied here, this is especially important with respect to the two military alliances in Europe – the North Atlantic Treaty Organization (NATO) and the Warsaw Treaty Organization (WTO).

A neutral policy also implies not taking an active part in international conflicts or war. But the use of foreign military sales as a means of recovering (part of) the costs for domestic military production may increase the possibility of a neutral becoming involved as a military supplier to one or more participants in an armed conflict. That possibility, we assume, increases with the number of recipients, especially if sales are directed toward politically unstable regions or countries.

An ideal outcome, such as the one represented by outcome A, reflects a strict and highly consistent implementation of a more restrictive formal policy. This Restraint outcome can be defined as follows:

- indigenous military production mainly for foreign customers does not exist;
- the value of global foreign military sales over time is on a constantly low level and/or is being reduced;
- the same is true of the number of recipients;

- with regard to geographical distribution, the government does not take advantage of the surge for military supplies in zones of armed conflict or high tension. There are no military sales to parties in conflict or war, not even to recipients in more generally defined conflict zones;
- military sales to members of NATO and the WTO are nonexistent or of little significance. If there are foreign military sales to alliance members, one could argue that sales to NATO and the WTO should be balanced to avoid criticism of favoring one of the two alliances; and
- in order to maximize neutral credibility, the major recipients of military supplies from the neutrals are other neutral countries.

Outcome A can be contrasted with outcome B (Legitimization), which represents a loose implementation of a formally more restrictive policy. This implies that the control requirements are not treated as absolute restrictions. Such an attitude can be a political benefit because it permits a certain freedom of action at the stage of implementation. References by the government to a 'total' view of all the relevant issues involved in each particular case should be expected, thereby reducing the importance of each individual control requirement. A more restrictive formal policy may in this case function as a 'silencer' of domestic and international opinion; the government expects that the secret aspects of formal policy, together with political confidence and trust, will keep public opinion content with formal policy. The public will remain uninterested and therefore unaware of foreign military sales, although actual sales may contradict all six conditions defined for outcome A.

Outcome B illustrates a major contradiction between formal foreign military sales policy and the implementation of that policy. It is highly unlikely that official attempts at secrecy will be successful in keeping the public uninformed; the contradiction itself between formal policy and actual foreign military sales can be expected to eventually create interest in foreign military sales both nationally and internationally. The result is a growing controversy between public demands for strict implementation of the control requirements and military-industrial-political brotherhood demands for a less restrictive formal policy.

Foreign military sales can also be used as a Domestic Policy Tool (outcome C). For small nations such as the neutrals, foreign military sales are normally not used as a *foreign* policy tool. Rather, foreign military sales are used to support domestic military production. As there are relatively fewer control requirements and/or less coverage by those requirements in this outcome than in outcome A, the *level* of actual foreign military sales (value and number of recipients) should be higher than in outcome A. Because implementation is strict, however, foreign military sales are not 'out of control'. The general foreign military sales *trends* ought therefore to be the same as for outcome A.

If, however, the government's attitude toward the relatively few control requirements is loose (outcome D), the situation is different. Such an attitude implies that whatever information is available is not necessarily taken into consideration when a foreign military sales decision is made. In comparison with outcome B, there are fewer and/or less coverage by the control requirements. In this outcome, foreign military sales are not treated much different from civilian sales. Foreign military sales become Business as Usual. This attitude also affects military production; it is of less importance if indigenous military production primarily fullfills domestic demands or demands by foreign customers.

Outcomes A and D are the most extreme outcomes in the REFORMIS approach. Outcome A reflects Restraint in foreign military sales, whereas in outcome D the distinction between military and civilian sales is largely unimportant. In outcome D, international competition becomes particularly important for the result in actual foreign military sales. In order to be successful, it is necessary to accept global market demands. Outcome A suggests the opposite; international competition is the least important among the four outcomes because actual sales are postulated to be low and/or reduced as a result of *national* policy. The other two outcomes are in between these extreme alternatives. International competition can be assumed to be relatively more important in outcome C than in outcome B, however, due to the less restrictive formal policy.

How can we take international competition into account when we analyze the actual results? It is impossible to be exact about the answer without detailed information about the competitive situation in each case of foreign military sales. Despite the difficulties, an attempt is made in section 5.2 to analyze the successes and failures of neutral states on the international military market. In general, it may be assumed that the broader the military industrial base and military R&D in a particular country, the greater are the chances for success on the international market. There are mainly two reasons for this. The first is that such a country has more military supplies to offer than does a country with a narrow military industrial base and with mainly license manufacture or only a few minor development projects. Second, such a country will generally have higher military expenses than will a nation with less military R&D projects. The government may therefore be more inclined to accept recipient demands in order to increase foreign military sales.

With this as a background, let us now study the situation for military production in each of the neutrals. This will give us an understanding of the military-industrial base in each country as well as the status of each country with regard to military R&D.

3

Modern History and
Military Buildup

One of the important differences among the neutrals is their war experience. Sweden and Switzerland managed to remain neutral during
World War II, while both Finland and Austria became actively
involved. Switzerland, although exposed to military threats, was the
only nation neighboring Germany which was not occupied by German
troops.

Neither Sweden nor Switzerland was involved in the drawing up
of treaties between victorious and defeated nations. As a result, military production and acquisitions in Sweden and Switzerland are in-
dependently defined by national policy. Military production and
acquisition in Finland and in Austria are to an important extent
circumscribed by treaties.

3.1   FINLAND

The Paris Peace Treaty in 1947 maximized Finland's Army to 34.400
troops, the Air Force to sixty aircraft and 3.000 troops, and the Navy
to 4.500 troops and a maximum weight of 10.000 tons (see Örvik 1979;
Möttölä 1984; Allison 1985). The following year Finland and the
Soviet Union signed the bilateral Treaty of Friendship, Cooperation
and Mutual Assistance (FCMA). It defines the military-political
relations between Finland and the Soviet Union. If a situation occurs in
which Finland may be used in ways that could threaten the security

interests of the Soviet Union, the treaty defines how the situation is to be handled by the two countries (*Handbok i Finlands säkerhetspolitik* 1984, p. 54; Hakovirta 1989). Finland is the only neutral which has established such formal relations with the Soviet Union. These relations have made Finland the only neutral with military trade with the Soviet Union.

'War materiel' is defined by the listing in Annex III of the Paris Peace Treaty. According to the second paragraph in the Treaty, the Allied and Associated Powers (the United Kingdom, Canada, Australia, New Zealand, India, Czechoslovakia, the Union of South Africa, the White-Russian and the Ukraine Socialist Republics, and the Soviet Union) can amend the list without the consent of the Finnish government. This is a special provision that has never been used.

Finland is not permitted to acquire all types of military materiel. The Treaty prohibits the acquisition of what was at the time considered offensive weapons or weapons of mass destruction, such as atomic weapons, assault (landing) craft, bombers and certain civilian aircraft, guided missiles, sea mines, torpedoes, submarines and motor torpedo boats. Military relations with Germany were likewise limited in both the Paris Peace Treaty and the FCMA. For instance, Finland was prohibited from acquiring war materiel of German origin (Maude 1976, p. 11).

But the Treaty went even further. It prohibited Finland from storing, acquiring or producing war materiel in excess of the needs of the armed forces as stipulated in the Treaty. Although not supposed to be permanent, these restrictions can be lifted only after permission from the signatory states has been obtained. And, indeed, so they have been, but in a protracted process. In 1962, Finland was allowed to modernize its forces with 'defensive' materiel such as Soviet surface-to-air missiles, Swedish-manufactured American air-to-air and Swedish-developed anti-ship missiles, all of which were imported. In 1983 Finland was also allowed to acquire certain types of sea mines (*Military Technology* 1986, no. 9, p. 170; *Ny Teknik*, July 24, 1986).

Finland, together with Sweden, is the only neutral with a Navy. Major ships are indigenously produced by Hollming and Wärtsilä. As noted, however, Finland does not have the right to acquire or produce submarines. Finland produces light (non-jet) aircraft of domestic design at the Valmet plant. Other major military production includes explosives and ammunition by Kemira, Vammaskoski, Forcit, Sako-Valmet, Tikkakoski and Lapua. Rifles and Army vehicles are produced by Valmet, mortars and field howitzers by Tampella, and electronics by Nokia and Strömberg.

3.2 AUSTRIA

The State Treaty for the Re-Establishment of an Independent and Democratic Austria was signed in May 1955 by the United States, the United Kingdom, France and the Soviet Union. The Treaty went into effect in July, and the foreign troops left the country in October of 1955. By means of a constitutional law passed that same month Austria became free, united and permanently neutral.

As a consequence of the State Treaty, as well as of the previous Paris Peace Treaty, military production and acquisition in Austria were restricted (Siegler, n.d., p. 158). Unlike the situation in Finland there are no maximum limits specified for the numbers of men and important military supplies in the Austrian Army. Nevertheless, because no changes have been made in the State Treaty by agreement with the signatories or with the U.N. Security Council, military acquisition has formally remained more restricted than in Finland.

Austria, like Finland, has been restricted in its acquisition of German military supplies. Although Austria agreed to dispose of German assets after the war, some German industrial plants were retained and formed the basis of Austria's military production after 1955. This was achieved after France, Great Britain and the United States refrained from all demands on German property (*Österrike* 1984). Although aircraft production was not continued in Austria after World War II, the Hermann Göring-Reichswerke was transformed into the Voest-Alpine AG. During the German occupation, Steyr was enlarged with the Niebelungenwerke, which is still part of the Steyr-Daimler-Puch group (Pilz 1987).

With the exception of Army materiel, most military materiel is manufactured under foreign license, and what Austria needs of other important supplies is imported. The State Treaty explicitly prohibits the production of rockets and guided missiles, guns with a range of more than thirty kilometers, and torpedoes (Article 13). Indigenous development is therefore heavily concentrated upon small arms and ammunition (produced by Hirtenberger Patronenfabrik, Armaturen GmbH, Ennstaler Metallwerke, Glock GmbH, Heinrich Ulbrichts WWe, and Südsteirische Metallindustrie), as well as upon mortars, guns and howitzers by Voest-Alpine AG and its subsidiary, Noricum. In addition, there is production of some optical and electronic equipment.

As in the case of Finland, air defense was for a long time virtually non-existent in Austria. Changes occurred during the late 1960s when Austria imported Swedish surplus aircraft as well as Swedish and Swiss anti-aircraft guns. During the 1970s, Austria also bought jet trainer aircraft from Sweden. An upgrading with missiles, however, as in Finland, has been prohibited by Article 13 of the State Treaty. The restrictions have been interpreted to include anti-aircraft missiles for even a minimal air defense (Schlesinger 1972, pp. 122-123) as well as missiles for anti-tank defense. While it is today common in many countries to acquire such missiles, Austria has attempted to compensate with the light tank. This type of equipment makes up a major part of Austrian military production. The SK-105 Küirassier (Panzerjäger) has been produced since 1970 by Steyer-Daimler-Puch (Pilz 1987).

The possible acquisition of missiles has become an important political and military issue in Austria. Opinion has been divided over whether or not to negotiate this issue with the signatories of the State Treaty (Defense & Armaments Heracles International, November 1987, p. 73). During 1988, however, the Defense Minister announced the acquisition of a small number of anti-tank missiles for 'training purposes'. This was done without prior permission of the signatories. The systems tested were the 'Milan 2', developed by France in cooperation with the Federal Republic of Germany, the American 'Dragon', and the Swedish 'Bill'. In June of 1989 it became known that the Swedish system had won the competition and that Austria had ordered, as the first foreign customer, an unknown number of missiles. Austria may also try to acquire a limited number of foreign air defense missiles during the 1990s (Jane's Defence Weekly, April 22, 1989, p. 695).

3.3   SWITZERLAND

Switzerland is not restricted in its attempts to arm. One of the most well-known producers is the privately owned Oerlikon-Bührle company with its Contraves subsidiary. Oerlikon is a major producer of anti-aircraft guns, ammunition and other Army supplies, including tanks. With the decision to license manufacture the German 'Leopard 2' heavy tank in Switzerland, production was transferred from the state-owned Konstruktionswerkstätte Thun (which produced an earlier tank) to Contraves. Light Army vehicles such as personnel carriers are indigenously produced by Motorwagenfabrik AG.

Important supplies such as the American F-5E 'Tiger' fighter aircraft and heavy guided missiles are imported or license manufactured. Modern non-jet trainer aircraft – which are important although they are not defined as war materiel by any of the neutrals as long as they are not armed – are produced by the Pilatus and FFA companies. The latter company is a subsidiary of the West German Dornier firm.

The Swiss manufacture of aircraft was broadened through the purchase in 1979 of the Britten-Norman aircraft company. Other military production includes electronics by Siemens, light arms by Schweizerische Industriegesellschaft and Waffenfabrik Bern and powder and ammunition by several producers.

3.4 SWEDEN

There are no international treaties limiting Sweden's military acquisitions. Successive Swedish governments since World War II have emphasized the importance of not becoming involved in any foreign military, economic or political relation that could seriously reduce Sweden's ability to decide over and implement national policies (Danckwardt & Hellman 1966; *Inriktningen av säkerhetspolitiken* 1977). This explains why Sweden has not accepted international neutrality guarantees.

During the second half of the 1930s, when Sweden requested important foreign supplies in order to quickly re-arm in response to the German military buildup, it was too late. Suppliers such as Great Britain, France and the United States would not sell. They knew or anticipated that they would soon be needing the goods themselves. One result was that Sweden had not received most of the advanced supplies on order when the war broke out. Another result was that the supplies which *were* received did not arrive in the quantities requested (Olsson 1977).

The official conclusion was that in order to avoid a repetition of 1939, indigenous R&D of military supplies were necessary. Sweden is the only neutral country with indigenous R&D in all categories of important materiel (guided missiles, fighter aircraft, surface ships, submarines and light as well as heavy tanks). As in the case of other major military producers, military R&D are done under increasing financial and technological constraints.

One of the most well-known Swedish suppliers is the Nobel Industrier with its Bofors subsidiary. Bofors is the major Swedish producer of anti-aircraft guns, ammunition and other Army supplies, including heavy tanks. Main suppliers of other Army vehicles are Hägglund & Söner, part of the ASEA group (light tanks and personnel carriers) and Volvo (personnel carriers and trucks). Sweden's naval production is not limited, as in Finland, to surface ships (produced by Karlskrona-varvet); production also includes conventionally powered submarines by Kockums. Fighter aircraft such as the 'Draken' and 'Viggen' series and jet trainers were developed and produced by Saab. At present Saab is developing the JAS39 'Gripen'. Since the completion of the Saab 'Safir' light aircraft series, advanced non-jet trainer aircraft have not been developed in Sweden. Air-to-ground and ground-to-air missiles, anti-ship missiles and anti-tank missiles are developed and produced by Saab and Bofors, individually or in cooperation. Among the main military producers is the state-owned FFV Ordnance (ammunition, handguns, rifles and light anti-tank weapons). The production of military electronics was rationalized during the 1980s by the acquisition of SATT and Philips Elektronikindustrier by Bofors. Bofors Electronics and Ericsson are today the two major producers of military electronics.

Despite the strong support of broad and advanced indigenous military R&D projects, all military acquisitions in Sweden are not the result of indigenous activities. Helicopters, Army support aircraft and light surface ships are imported, as are air-to-air missiles and heavy air defense missiles. Jet engines for all of Sweden's fighter aircraft are license manufactured by Volvo Flygmotor. Much of the production of electronic parts and components is, moreover, based upon foreign know-how.

3.5   COMPARISONS

Gross Industrial Indicators

Table 3.1 illustrates some of the characteristics of the neutral countries discussed previously. With regard to defense expenditures during the 1980s one can separate the neutrals into pairs: Austria and Finland, on the one hand, and Sweden and Switzerland, on the other. The latter pair spends two to three times as much per capita on defense as does the former pair. Although less pronounced, these pair similarities also stand out with regard to the share of government spending.

But size is not the only explanation of these differences. World War II experiences and the post-war peace treaties resulted in different armament 'rhythms'. The governments in Sweden and Switzerland were not restricted by such treaties, and their pre-war economies and industrial structures remained intact. They were convinced that armed neutrality was a workable solution and defined security to a large extent in military terms. Austria and Finland were restricted in their military acquisitions and therefore emphasized the political aspects of security.

TABLE 3.1
Comparison of military variables

Country	Mn U.S.$ (current)			Public Defense Expenditures U.S.$/cap.			% of gvnt. spending			% of GDP/GNP			Public Military R&D (mn U.S.$) (1980 prices)			
	1980	1982	1984	1980	1982	1984	1980	1982	1984	1980	1984	1986	1980	1982	1983	1986
Austria	952	833	792	127	110	106	4.0	3.8	3.6	1.2	1.2	1.3	1.5	1.5	-	-
Finland	734	809	815	154	168	168	5.4	5.7	5.7	1.4	1.6	2.1	5.4	6.3	6.5	7.1
Sweden	3867	2840	2862	465	341	341	8.0	7.3	7.2	3.3	3.0	2.5	228.6	246.4	311.3	387.1
Switzerland	2108	2036	1958	330	314	301	20.3	21.4	21.3	2.1	2.1	1.9	50.4	-	-	-

Sources: Based on data from World Armaments and Disarmament; The Military Balance; and Sivard.

Sweden and Switzerland have maintained continuous re-armament policies since 1945. Finland, however, 'hesitated' until the 1960s. This can be explained by three factors: The restrictions put on Finland's military acquisitions; Finland's war debt and the conversion of several wartime military industries to civilian activities, which led to reduced military production after 1945; and the change of rhythm during the 1960s, which signaled the beginning of a modernization of the armed forces in general and air defense in particular.

With regard to Austria it can be debated whether it has developed an armament rhythm at all. Military production was for a long time concentrated in small arms and ammunition. Not until the 1970s did Steyr-Daimler-Puch and Voest-Alpine expand their production to include armored vehicles and artillery (Brzoska & Ohlson 1987, p. 105). The Austrian military industry then underwent what researchers at SIPRI called 'somewhat of a revival' (*World Armaments and Disarmament* 1983, p. 282). As will be shown, however (Chapter 4), this revival was short. It seems to have been only a temporary oscillation, not the beginning of an armament rhythm.

Finland is the only neutral in which the defense share of gross domestic product/gross national product (GDP/GNP) has constantly increased during the 1980s. This is to say that defense has been favorably treated in relation to other public expenditures. In Austria the share has remained relatively stable, while in Switzerland it has recently decreased.

Sweden, in direct contrast to Finland, experienced a continued decrease in defense spending during the early 1980s. Roughly the same general directions – upward trends in Finland and constant or downward trends in the other three neutrals – can be noted for the other variables. With regard to military production as a share of GNP/GDP (table 3.2), there has been no drastic year-by-year variations with the exception of Austria. Only Sweden and Switzerland have a share greater than 1 per cent, reflecting relatively more and larger indigenous development and manufacturing projects than in Austria and Finland.

Sweden's relatively stable curve reflects its broader military production base with more ongoing projects than in the other countries. This fits the conclusion from table 3.1, as well as the relatively high military share of Swedish industrial production (table 3.3). The increase in Switzerland in 1982 can be explained by the manufacture of the Leopard tank and increasing foreign military sales (see Chapter 4). The slight increase in the military share of Swedish industrial production in 1979 and 1980 is explained mainly by production for foreign customers (see Chapter 4).

TABLE 3.2
Military production: Share of GNP/GDP, 1978-1986 (%)*

Country	1978	1979	1980	1981	1982	1983	1984	1985	1986
Austria	.9	.6	.4	.6	.4	.4	.3	-	-
Finland	.1	.2	.2	.2	.2	.2	.2	.2	-
Sweden	1.2	1.3	1.3	1.2	1.2	1.1	1.1	1.1	-
Switzerland	.7	.7	.7	.8	1.0	1.2	1.0	1.2	1.1

* Some countries use GNP, others GDP. Because the shares are very low, the use of either/or does not influence the results to any significant degree.

Sources: Austria: estimates by Peter Pilz using company annual reports; Finland: calculations by Pertti Joenniemi; Sweden: FMV annual reports, official Swedish war materiel sales statistics and Swedish foreign trade statistics; calculations by the author with the assistance of Leif Hedberg (National Defense Research Institute); Switzerland: calculations by Peter Hug.

TABLE 3.3
Military production: Share of total industrial production of goods, 1978-1985 (%)

Country	1978	1979	1980	1981	1982	1983	1984	1985
Austria	1.9	1.2	.7	1.2	.8	.9	.7	-
Finland	.2	.2	.2	.2	.2	.2	.2	.2
Sweden	2.1	2.2	2.2	2.1	2.0	1.9	1.8	1.8

Sources: See table 3.2 and explanations in the text.

The statistical uncertainties included in these figures should be emphasized. Although a fairly reliable figure for GNP or GDP can be found in each country, this is not the case for military production and industrial production. For the latter there are different variables depending upon the type of industrial production. Table 3.3 is based on national statistics for industrial production of goods (manufacture). Strangely enough, no such breakdown of production has been found for Switzerland. It has therefore been left out of table 3.3.

Another difficulty concerns the definition of military production. Because there are no readily available figures, it has been necessary to combine different figures in table 3.2. The method has been to use, when available, a figure for total government military purchases, subtracting from that the value of direct military imports and adding the value of military exports. Although none of these individual figures is easily identified, they have been considered reliable enough to permit gross comparisons.

For Austria there are particular problems. There are no published official figures for military production or foreign military sales. Instead, they have been estimated from available company reports. This means that the statistics for Austria should be treated with more care than the figures for the other countries.

The generally low values in tables 3.2 and 3.3 indicate that reduced military production need not in general cause drastic economic difficulties for the societies as a whole. In nations where domestic industrial production is narrow or where military production is highly specialized, such reductions may nevertheless affect national indicators. This is illustrated by Austria. In 1978 the military share of industrial production was about the same in Austria and Sweden. In Austria this was largely made up of the production of equipment for the Army by Voest-Alpine and Steyr-Daimler-Puch. Due to reduced orders at home and abroad (Pilz 1987), the military share of industrial production in Austria declined to less than 1 per cent. For Sweden the reduction has been smaller, which reflects both a broader production base and different foreign recipients (see Chapter 4).

Several nations and major firms have had to adapt themselves to increasing costs of military production. The neutral nation which has had to adapt the least is Finland. The most important explanation seems to be that there has been public support for (relatively high budget allocations for) domestic military acquisitions. The domestic military market in Finland has not declined to the same extent as in the other neutral countries (Möttölä 1984, p. 132).

Furthermore, materiel expenses in Finland have been directed to specific and limited areas of modernization. During the 1970s the main beneficiary was air defense; during the 1980s the Army was favored. This modernization has taken place through a mixture of indigenous development, license manufacture and direct imports, all of which have limited technological risk as well as production cost.

Military R&D

The differences among the neutrals in table 3.1 are most clearly marked with regard to public expenditures for military R&D. It should be noted that figures for public R&D do not include private financing by the industries themselves or by foreign sources. It is not possible to define the exact magnitude of such funding. It is clear, however, that the figures underestimate the total value of military R&D, especially in Sweden and Switzerland.

Even though Austria and Finland show the lowest expenditures, the gap is fairly wide between the two. Finland shows more than three times the expenditure for military R&D as Austria does. Three explanations for this gap are suggested. First, the Austrian Army has traditionally not used the latest, and therefore not the most expensive technology. Second, Austrian treaty restrictions have limited the acquisition options more than has occurred in Finland. The costs have therefore been relatively low. Third, there is relatively more license manufacture in Austria compared to more indigenous (and often more expensive) development of military materiel in Finland.

Austria, Finland and Switzerland are in a separate category when compared to publicly financed military R&D in Sweden. This was very clearly presented in a SIPRI study of the pattern of R&D during the 1960s. SIPRI drew the 'threshold line' at a defense budget between $500 and $700 million per year. None of the countries below the line, including Austria, Finland and Switzerland, devoted more than 1.5 per cent of total public military expenditures to R&D (*World Armaments and Disarmament* 1972, pp. 161-62; see also *Resources Devoted to Military Research and Development* 1972). This was explained by the relative importance of imports as opposed to indigenous R&D of major weapons by those three nations. The scale of their overall military effort was small. Major development projects were limited to a few types of equipment with a history of indigenous development, such as non-jet aircraft in Finland and Switzerland and armored vehicles in Austria and Switzerland.

The SIPRI study placed Sweden above the dividing line (military expenditures of $700 million or more per year). It should be noted that this was at a time when Sweden had an exceptionally high number of important ongoing R&D projects. With regard to the Swedish position vis-à-vis the other neutrals, the description is still accurate. Military R&D expenses increased during the 1980s due to the development of the new fighter aircraft JAS39 'Gripen' and increasing research in anti-submarine warfare (*Forskningsstatistik* 1985/86, 1987).

Official data on public expenditures for military R&D including tests in Switzerland indicate that the expenditures were stabilized between $50 and $60 million until 1986. They then increased to more than $100 million (information from P. Hug). Because the figure includes tests, it is not possible to draw the conclusion that military R&D in Switzerland has doubled. Sweden's special position can therefore be assumed to still be true.

Public and Private Ownership

There are also differences among the neutrals with regard to the
ownership of military production. Most of the military producers in
Austria are state-owned (public) companies. The primary argument for
nationalization in Austria was that only the state could raise enough
capital to re-create industrial production after World War II. In the
other three countries the situation is mixed, albeit in different ways.
There seems to be no common denominator to explain the total distribution between private and public companies; the distribution is most
likely the result of historical and economic circumstances[1].

Much military production in Finland is public, such as the production of light arms and ammunition as well as aircraft production by
Valmet. In Sweden aircraft production by Saab, like most military
production, is performed by private firms. Only FFV and the major
shipyards Kockums and Karlskronavarvet are publicly owned. In
contrast, naval production in Finland is private. The one common denominator is that the major Army producers – Bofors, Volvo and
Hägglund & Söner in Sweden; Oerlikon-Bührle in Switzerland; and
Tampella in Finland – are privately owned. Private production in
Switzerland was strengthened with the manufacture of the Leopard
tank by Oerlikon-Bührle.

In general, there seems to be a development toward increasing com-
mercialization in the behavior of military firms. This development is
visible in Sweden and Finland and may become more important in
Switzerland.

Internationalization of Military Production

Military production is mainly based in the neutral countries themselves. This is to say that the neutrals have generally not penetrated
the international military market by way of extensive direct investments in military production abroad. Although several of the
military producers belong to multinational industrial groups, their
major foreign activities do not involve military production. When
they decide to invest abroad, the purpose may instead be to increase
marketing and sales activities. Judging from an official Swedish study

---

[1]In Switzerland public companies are 'state military enterprises' and as such
are part of the public administration. The workers are appointed as Civil
Servants. Usually, these companies do not export war materiel (information
from P. Hug).

in 1986 thirteen out of seventeen Swedish military producers with foreign subsidiaries (in which they controlled at least 20 per cent of the capital) had mainly marketing functions. Only three companies were involved in military development and/or manufacture abroad: Ericsson in Norway and Italy, Bofors in Singapore, and Kockums in Australia (*Försvarsindustrins utlandsverksamhet* 1987, p. 48; annual company reports).

Sweden is the largest military producer among the four neutrals. Production in Sweden is performed mostly by private firms. Because military production abroad is not controlled by the government, it could be assumed that Swedish producers would try the hardest to take advantage of the possibilities for military industrial activities abroad. Thus, if Swedish foreign military investments abroad are low, they probably are also low for the other neutrals. Available information indicates this to be generally true. There is one outstanding exception, however: Oerlikon-Bührle. It seems to be the only military producer in the neutral countries with important military production abroad. Sampson noted that during the 1970s Oerlikon-Bührle produced more weapons abroad than in Switzerland (Sampson 1978, p. 298). In the 1980s a majority of its employees were still working abroad (Hug 1987).

In general, however, most foreign production of military equipment is performed through license manufacture by foreign companies. This manufacture can be assumed to be of rather large proportions. By 1986 Swedish military firms had close to seventy license manufacturing agreements in force around the world. Some of them were quite old, and most were for weapons and/or ammunition (*Försvarsindustrins utlandsverksamhet* 1987). It can be assumed that the other neutrals have also sold a large number of military manufacturing licenses to foreign customers, although the full extent of such sales is unknown. According to SIPRI, by 1986 Switzerland had sold more manufacturing licenses for important materiel to Third World recipients than had either Austria or Sweden (Brzoska & Ohlson 1987; *World Armaments and Disarmament* 1987, 1988). Together with additional national information it seems that important Swiss materiel has been manufactured in Argentina and Chile (personnel carriers), the Philippines (light aircraft), Indonesia (missiles) and South Korea, Brazil, Turkey and India (anti-aircraft systems). During recent years Switzerland has sold manufacturing rights to Australia (light aircraft) and the United States (ADATS air defense system). Austria has sold the rights to Nigeria and Greece to manufacture armed personnel carriers and to Greece to manufacture howitzers. In 1974 Sweden sold a license to Pakistan for the manufacture of light trainer aircraft. During the 1980s Sweden sold the right to India to manufacture howitzers and to Australia to manufacture anti-aircraft missiles and submarines.

Another important mode of production is cooperation in a particular project between companies in the neutral countries and foreign firms (*ad hoc* cooperation). About sixty international cooperative agreements involving Swedish military producers were in force in 1986 (*Försvarsindustrins utlandsverksamhet* 1987). Although this figure may be an exaggeration and probably includes many small and limited projects – because it is difficult to clearly define military industrial cooperation and because the companies themselves may define as much activity as possible as cooperation because this mode is excluded from Swedish foreign military sales control requirements – *ad hoc* cooperation seems more common than direct financial investment in military production abroad. Nevertheless, *ad hoc* cooperation has not yet become as common as foreign license manufacture.

The internationalization of military production has important future consequences for foreign military sales. For instance, European producers in countries which are not members of the EC have, in view of the planned common market in 1992, made deliberate attempts to get a foothold inside the EC. These attempts have mainly taken the form of acquisitions of foreign companies. A recent Swedish study suggested that during the 1980s there was a break in the traditional policy of Swedish multinational firms of centralizing R&D in the home country. Although the twenty groups included in the study were mainly civilian producers, important military producers such as Ericsson, Nobel Industrier, Saab-Scania and Volvo were included (*Forskning och utveckling i utlandet* 1989).

To summarize: there are certain similarities and differences with regard to neutral military industrial structure, production and acquisition. World War II experiences and treaties drawn up after the war have left basic differences between Austria and Finland, on the one hand, and Sweden and Switzerland, on the other. The former, having been directly involved in the war and therefore parties to peace treaties, are restricted in their military production and acquisitions. Sweden and Switzerland are free to decide on their own. The common policy of neutrality as such has not reduced these basic differences.

In Austria, most military production was nationalized after World War II; the other countries have retained a mixture of private and public ownership. Direct investment in military production abroad is rare; the only exception is Switzerland's Oerlikon-Bührle. Foreign military sales from foreign companies, partly or wholly owned by companies in the neutral countries, seem in general quite limited. It companies in the neutral countries, seem in general quite limited. It should therefore not complicate present neutral foreign military sales statistics. For the future, however, this is a mode of trade that should be closely watched.

Nevertheless, international *ad hoc* cooperation and foreign license manufacture are important modes of trade not covered by neutral foreign military sales statistics. This is a serious drawback that is covered only to a limited extent by other, complementary statistical sources. We will return to this issue later.

Economic support for the domestic military market has differed among the neutrals. Only in Finland has there been enough support to balance, or at least counter, cost increases. In all of the other neutrals the domestic market has decreased. In accordance with the REFORMIS approach, this decrease can be expected to increase the military-industrial-political demand for foreign military sales, especially in countries with large and advanced military production. We can therefore assume that among the neutrals there is relatively stronger support for foreign military sales in Sweden and Switzerland than in Austria and Finland. This will be especially true for Sweden due to its R&D of more advanced military supplies. Because the financial support of military acquisition in Finland has been strong, there ought to be less of an economic need in Finland for foreign military sales than in the other neutrals.

In Chapter 4 we will analyze if and how the domestic situations have affected the formal policy. In Chapter 5 we will analyze actual foreign military sales from the neutrals.

4

Foreign Military Sales

4.1 FORMAL POLICY: NUMBER AND COVERAGE OF RESTRICTIVE REQUIREMENTS

Table 4.1 compares the number and coverage of neutral foreign military sales control requirements. The number of requirements is defined as the number of years in which new foreign military sales legislation was enacted (i.e., year of legislation). The change of an old requirement is identified as a new requirement. By coverage is meant the content of the requirements. The number of requirements and their coverage reflect the relative restrictiveness of military sales policy; the more control requirements and the wider their coverage, the more restrictive the policy.

It is evident that Sweden and Switzerland have the largest number of control requirements of the four neutrals. Aside from unconditional requirements, control requirements include end-use certificates (a written declaration by the recipient not to re-transfer the materiel without the consent of the supplying government) and no sales to governments violating human rights. There are differences between the two countries, however, as well as between the other neutrals. Although Switzerland has a relatively large number of control requirements, their total coverage is not broader than the much fewer requirements in Austria and Finland. Sweden has certain requirements that do not exist in any of the other neutrals – for instance, the prohibition of military training of foreigners in Sweden unless it is a part of war materiel sales; the requirement of an export license for the granting of manufacturing rights abroad; the requirement of government or police permission to work as an intermediary in foreign military sales; and some explicit guidelines concerning Swedish participation in international military industrial cooperation. Although Swedish war materiel sales to countries involved in armed conflict are prohibited, certain sales are nevertheless permitted. Sales of spare parts and ammunition in order to complete previous orders are allowed even to countries involved in war. Similarly, trade between Swedish and foreign companies or government institutions involved in cooperative projects are excluded from the conditional control requirements.

Neither in Austria nor in Switzerland are sales of spare parts or ammunition to a country in armed conflict accepted under any circumstance. The regulations in Finland are not clear on this point. In Finland and Austria end-use certificates are not demanded in every military sale, but such is the case in Sweden and Switzerland. There is a principle in Sweden and Finland not to produce military materiel purely for exports. This principle does not exist in Switzerland or Austria. Finland has no requirement which prohibits sales to a government violating human rights. In the case of Sweden sales are allowed to governments violating human rights as long as Swedish materiel is not used in the violations. With the exception of Sweden, no neutral government today stipulates controls of intermediaries in international military trade.

TABLE 4.1
Formal foreign military sales control requirements and sanction mechanisms

Nation	Year of Legislation	Unconditional Requirements	Countries in Conflict	Conflict Regions	Violation of Human Rights	End-use Certificates	Marketing Activities and Sales Offers	Production Only for Export
Austria	1977 1982	Membership of international organizations or international agreements	Sales prohibited		Sales prohibited 1982	Selective use		
Finland	1985 1986	See above	Sales prohibited	Sales prohibited		Selective use		Restricted i principle
Sweden	1950 1967 1971 1982 1984 1988	See above	Sales prohibited	Sales prohibited	Sales prohibited if Swedish materiel is used	Always since 1983; from 1988 with involvement of Swedish authorities in recipient country	Information demanded since 1988	Controlled
Switzerland	1946 1949 1972 1973 1978 1980	See above	Sales prohibited	Sales prohibited	Sales prohibited	Always since 1949		

* In most cases this also means a violation of the neutrality law, resulting in max 5 years imprisonment.

The basis for the conditional control requirements is the definition and use of the term *war materiel*. One distinction that exists in Sweden is between 'defensive' and 'offensive' materiel. In general, the requirements are less restrictive for defensive than for other types of supplies. This distinction has a long tradition. It was noted previously that Finland in 1962 and 1983 was allowed to modernize its forces with defensive weapons. This was also an important consideration in Austria's recent first-time decision to buy anti-tank missiles.

In Sweden the distinction has been used for materiel such as anti-aircraft and coastal artillery as well as mines. After 1983, however, the importance of this distinction should, according to a parliamentary decision, have been reduced when allowing foreign military sales. Experiences from Indonesia/East Timor, Burma (Myanmar) and other conflicts involving Swedish war materiel have shown that the distinction is not sufficiently clarifying; it is as much a matter of the operative use of a weapon in actual combat as of the technical drawing-board specifications. The distinction can nevertheless still be used in Sweden to permit sales (*Regeringens proposition* 1982).

Only in Sweden is the sale of manufacturing rights (license agreements) included in the control requirements. All Swedish military license agreements signed before 1983 (when the recent export law came into effect) and still in force were investigated in 1988. It was

Conditional requirements							
Manufacturing Licenses	Military Training of Foreigners	Offensive/ Defensive Weapons	Re-transfer of War Materiel	Intermediaries	Cooperation with Industries Abroad	Subsidiaries Abroad/Shares in Foreign Industries	Punishment
			Controlled				Max imprisonment 2 years*
			Controlled				
Permit needed	Not permitted in Sweden if not part of foreign military sale; always permitted abroad	Distinction in use	Controlled	Partly controlled	No conditional controls, but under political supervision	Shall be reported to the government	Max imprisonment 4 years
			Controlled				Max imprisonment 5 years

Sources: Information from P. Hug, P. Joenniemi, P. Pilz, A. Truger and the author.

found that only a few of them prevented the re-transfer by the licensee of either the manufactured goods or the know-how itself (*Press Release* 1988b). Because license sales were not included in the control requirements before 1983, this situation was not fully known to the Swedish government. This illustrates both the importance of well-defined control requirements and the use of license agreements as a possible way to circumvent other control requirements.

Definitions and conceptual distinctions can be added or excluded in ways that change the list of war materiel. This is not the same as changing the control requirements. The most important distinction is the one between military and civilian materiel. It defines, by exclusion, the list of war materiel. Swedish changes in export regulations since the 1960s have, for instance, excluded types of materiel from the control requirements by neglecting to define them as 'specifically designed for military use' (Hagelin 1985). This is the definition of war materiel used by all the neutrals. Almost every category of materiel, apart from armored vehicles, weapons and ammunition, has a civilian counterpart which needs no export permit. Examples are unarmed vehicles (ships, ground vehicles, aircraft), radar and other electronic equipment, small caliber arms and ammunitions for hunting or target practice and standard goods.

This raises the question about 'strategic' or 'dual use' supplies, i.e., civilian goods, services and know-how with a possible military use. Although not included in the official definitions of war materiel by the neutrals, such goods are sometimes included in international statistical compilations. The Western export embargo toward Communist countries after World War II illustrates the importance of both strategic goods and the position of the neutrals in Western policy toward Communist countries.

The term *strategic good* originated in the United States when it embargoed such goods to Communist countries from 1945 on. In order for this embargo to be effective, however, other nations had to become involved and had to accept the same or similar export control requirements. The result was CoCom, the informal Consultative Committee, established during the late 1940s. It included the OEEC countries with the exception of Iceland and Japan.

The neutrals presented a particular problem. They traded with countries in both the East and the West. Being neutral, they could not officially accept the embargo policy dictated by Western political interests against a specific group of nations. Finland created, as part of its national economic policy, trade controls toward the Soviet Union which were acceptable to the U.S. government. For the other three countries, however, the issue was more complicated and more sensitive. The negotiations between those countries and the United States were secret – had they become known at the time, neutral credibility would have suffered a severe blow. Switzerland in 1951 accepted the embargo system by signing the Holz-Linder agreement (Hug 1987). In 1961 J. Behrman, Acting U.S. Assistant Secretary of Commerce for International Affairs, stated in a secret congressional hearing that there were already sufficient re-transfer controls in both Finland and Switzerland (*Export of Strategic Materials* 1961, pp. 135-136).

Austria and Sweden had informally followed the Western control restrictions. With changing political relations between the United States and the Soviet Union during the early 1980s, U.S. pressures increased. Austria formally accepted strategic re-transfer controls in 1984 (Luif 1985). Sweden was last among the neutrals, passing a similar law in 1986 (*Press Release* 1986).

Despite these developments, all the neutrals have avoided the inclusion of dual-use supplies in their definitions of war materiel. The range of supplies included in such controls would clearly be wider than the present definitions of war materiel. In accordance with the REFORMIS approach, governments try to avoid decisions that could complicate or put military production and sales at risk. Their refusals to broaden the definition of war materiel support this thesis.

One clear example is the reasoning in Sweden before the decision in 1985 to extend the embargo toward South Africa (Hagelin 1988, pp. 165-166). The Swedish government has not allowed war materiel sales to that country for more than twenty-five years. Sweden followed U.N. recommendations against sales to South Africa long before the mandatory embargo in 1977. The U.N. standpoint, plus strong national and international critique in general of the apartheid system, led the Swedish government to accept unilateral actions against South Africa although they went contrary to Swedish commercial interests.

In 1977 the Swedish Parliament imposed a law prohibiting the sale of war materiel as well as inventions of war materiel and similar know-how for both military and police use to South Africa. In 1985 the war materiel embargo was extended to include computers, computer programs, vehicles and gasoline, supplies which were not otherwise included in the list of war materiel. Although there is no comprehensive Swedish trade boycott, *all* trade with South Africa has required a government license since 1986.

At the same time, the Swedish government did not impose the most extensive controls possible even toward South Africa. To redefine war materiel as materiel 'of military importance', which would have been in accordance with the U.N. decision, was found by a Swedish investigation to be impractical. Furthermore, such a redefinition could hamper Sweden's trade with other countries. These conclusions were accepted by the government, and a broad definition of war materiel was subsequently rejected (*Med förslag till lag* 1984).

A definition of war materiel including all materiel bought or used by South African military and police agencies was found to be broader than what was suggested by the United Nations. The definition was therefore not considered necessary. The Swedish government eventually decided to add certain materiel to the embargo that was not on the Swedish war materiel list. It was emphasized that this was not a general extension of the Swedish war materiel list and would not apply to any country other than South Africa.

This example illustrates that the Swedish government recognized that it is insufficient to prohibit only the sale of war materiel, as presently defined, if foreign armament is to be effectively controlled. That the controls applied to South Africa have not been imposed on all Swedish foreign military sales also show that South Africa is a special case. In addition, the decision may indicate that the military and industrial interests against a general broadening of the war materiel sales list were regarded as more legitimate than the demand for a total military embargo.

According to the REFORMIS approach, the sooner control requirements were introduced after World War II, and the more such requirements were added since then, the more aware and concerned the public has been of the foreign military sales issue and the more willing the government has been to accept public demands for further control requirements. Although all the neutrals have formulated new foreign military sales control requirements since 1945, only Sweden and Switzerland were quick to do so. Table 4.1 shows that most control requirements were introduced during the 1970s and 1980s. This suggests that some general conditions may have influenced the introduction of control requirements in all of the neutrals. Let us look at such general conditions before discussing the more specific factors.

The years from 1945 can be divided into three periods. The ten years between 1945 and 1955 were marked by the rebuilding of Europe. The effects of the peace treaties on the military production in Austria and Finland as well as on their military acquisitions were described previously. Only Sweden and Switzerland were free to decide about their military production. The increasing political and military tension between East and West in general and the United States and the Soviet Union in particular, however, involved most Western European nations in the U.S. attempts to control military and strategic trade. Political factors can therefore be assumed to be important in explaining the first control requirements by Switzerland and Sweden.

The second period, from 1955 to the early 1970s, included the height of the cold war as well as its erosion. Military production began in Austria after 1955, and the political constraints from the first period were eased during the 1960s. Around that time decolonization was begun. Together, these developments gave more room for small states in international politics. The new nation-states – the 'developing countries' or 'Third World' – had military demands which generally fit military production in the neutral countries better than did the military demands from the major industrialized powers. It was during this period that international possibilities for increasing foreign military sales from the neutrals occurred.

This period also included the height of the Vietnam war and the subsequent U.S. withdrawal. The Vietnam War was a stimulus to U.S. and other national peace movements. After the U.S. withdrawal from Vietnam, many of these movements turned to other peace-related issues. One was to oppose nuclear armaments and to demand international arms control. A related issue was the control of global arms trade.

The second period thus created possibilities for increasing foreign military sales from smaller nations as well as an increasing public preparedness for that particular issue. This was the period of new military breakthroughs – for instance, the transistor and the 'chip' with never-before-anticipated effects upon miniaturization and computerization – with cost increases as one result. More suppliers also resulted in increasing international competition and new modes of trade. These developments stimulated debates about military issues in general and demands for increasing foreign military sales in particular. Public awareness was stimulated by the activities of peace movements as well as by the increasing availability of information about foreign military sales. The major international information sources (such as ACDA and SIPRI) were first published during this period. This created new possibilities for continual surveillance of global foreign military sales.

International possibilities for increasing foreign military sales, new and expensive military technologies, the appearance of more suppliers, increasing national demands for foreign military sales and increasing public awareness of the issue together with increasing visibility of foreign military sales made the neutral dilemma appear during the second period. This may explain why there have generally been more new control requirements introduced during the third period, which began in the mid-1970s, than before. With this as a background we can turn to the specific situation in each neutral country.

Sweden has enacted a relatively continual series of new control requirements since 1945. They also have the broadest coverage. The first Swedish change was not, however, the result of public demands. Instead, it was mainly a political response to new military technologies developed during the war. This, as well as indications that the U.S. CoCom negotiations may have been important (Hagelin 1985), illustrate the heavy Swedish focus upon technologically advanced military supplies.

Likewise, Switzerland was quick to introduce new requirements. In Switzerland the change in 1949 was more of a compromise between public opinion demands for a strict implementation of the 1946 ban on foreign military sales and brotherhood demands for foreign military sales (Hug 1987).

This differs from the other neutrals, where new requirements were not introduced until the 1970s or 1980s and for which the coverage is still limited. In Finland certain electronics were included in the definition of war materiel in 1985, and selective end-use certificates were introduced in 1986. In Austria a special law on military sales was adopted in 1977, and in 1982 a clause was introduced forbidding exports to states violating human rights.

Among the neutrals, Sweden therefore stands out as special with regard to formal policy. This can be explained by several factors. First, the peace treaties concluded by Finland and Austria indirectly restricted foreign military sales by limiting military production. It is therefore possible that nationally imposed restrictions have not been regarded as equally important in Austria and Finland as in Sweden and Switzerland.

Second, it is suggested that public debates about military and security issues have been more frequent and more successful in influencing policy in Sweden than in any of the other neutral countries. This is explained not only by unique factors; the combination of factors is probably just as important. One unique factor was the opposition to plans to acquire Swedish atomic weapons during the 1950s and 1960s. Those who were involved in that debate are eager to conclude that it was because of their actions that the Swedish government in 1966 decided not to acquire such weapons. A recent study reached a somewhat different conclusion, namely, that a change also occurred within the Swedish Armed Forces based upon a military cost/risk-benefit analysis (Agrell 1985).

The active youth organizations of the political parties are another important factor. They have generally been more radical than the political parties. Because Sweden has for a long time been governed by the Social Democratic party, the Social Democratic Youth (SSU) has been of particular importance. It conducted a three-month campaign in 1968 which included a critique of Sweden's military sales to Latin America (Andersson & Stenquist 1988, ch. 1). This action was a step toward the new requirements in 1971.

These developments created important national basis for public critique. Several individuals involved in the atomic weapons and/or the Latin American debates continued to be active as individuals, as members of peace organizations or as members of Parliament. With regard to developments during the 1980s, foreign military sales were taken up as a special issue by the Swedish Peace and Arbitration Society (SPAS) in 1983. SPAS was created in 1883 and is one of the world's oldest peace organizations (Fogelström 1971). The main reason for devoting special attention to military sales in 1983 was the public debate over that issue which had begun in 1979. Since 1974 SPAS has published its present journal, *Pax*, which has been an important source of information for other peace movements and activists as well as for the interested general public. Different mass media have also been important in publicizing SPAS information, especially between 1983 and 1986.

In summary, since the 1950s, organizations as well as individuals from different sections of Swedish society have appeared presenting arguments, attitudes and information concerning foreign military sales. Due to the central involvement of SPAS, as well as alleged illegal sales, the issue received broader media coverage during the 1980s than before. Also important is the involvement of the SSU and the fact that several members of Parliament have a background in public action and peace movements. They have frequently picked up on the foreign military sales issue and kept it alive in Parliament.

As a consequence, and in order to put the Swedish control requirements in perspective, it should be noted that most of the requirements were recently introduced. The demand for end-use certificates, introduced as a mandatory requirement in Switzerland at the end of the 1940s, became obligatory in Sweden only in 1983. Also, the requirement of an export license for the sale of manufacturing rights had been demanded long before it was accepted in 1983. This indicates that the stubborn repetition of demands may eventually give an issue legitimacy and result in political acceptance.

In 1988 the Swedish control requirements were strengthened as a reaction to the alleged illegal sales during the early and mid-1980s. The new requirements include stronger end-use as well as new end-manufacturing requirements. The government must be informed about marketing activities and sales offers to foreign governments. The control requirements for manufacturing rights abroad now apply to all firms and individuals, not only to previously defined military producers. Agreements involving the development of war materiel in Sweden for a foreign customer require government acceptance. The controls over intermediaries were also strengthened, and Swedish shares in foreign military firms must now be reported (*Press Release* 1988a). Thus, the government must be informed by the military producers about a variety of *pre*-sale actions.

Switzerland is the neutral country which is most similar to Sweden with regard to the number of control requirements. Nevertheless, it has been difficult to obtain exact information of the total number of changes in Swiss formal policy after World War II. It may be that the number of control requirements is higher in Switzerland than in Sweden. Even so, the main conclusions are not seriously affected.

Foreign military sales from Switzerland quickly became a public issue after World War II. There have been several public debates about war materiel sales in Switzerland (Hug 1987). As in Sweden, the existence of a peace movement, including specialized journals such as *Friedenspolitik* and *Friedenszeitung*, has kept the public informed and has helped to create awareness and concern for the foreign military sales issue.

But why do the control requirements in Switzerland have a more narrow coverage than in Sweden, although the number of requirements is the same? The answer is that subsequent requirements have added only small changes to the previous requirements in Switzerland. This could indicate that public demands for a more restrictive policy have not been able to break through a basic official laissez-faire attitude. The broad coverage of the control requirements in Sweden could, by the same reasoning, be explained by an official Swedish attitude in support of more involvement in economic affairs.

There is yet another important difference between Sweden and Switzerland. Switzerland is the one example among the neutral countries where there exists an explicit political decision to implement formal policy loosely. In 1978 a resolution was adopted by both chambers of Parliament asking the government to interpret the law in a *less* restrictive way (Brzoska & Ohlson 1987, p. 110). This decision fits the laissez-faire attitude and suggests that subsequent restrictive demands are less likely to be accepted.

In both Austria and Finland public debates have occurred at a relatively recent date. Public awareness and concern in Austria parallel increasing military production and sales. Debates following sales of Austrian war materiel to the Middle East and South America resulted in new Austrian control requirements in 1977. The planned sale of the Küirassier light tank to Chile in 1980 received only waivering political support and eventually resulted in the adoption of further control requirements in 1982 (*World Armaments and Disarmament* 1981, p. 196; Pilz 1982). Allegations of illegal sales to Iran and Iraq during the Gulf war have resulted in discussions within the government about increasing foreign military sales restrictions (*Milavnews*, Austria, AAS-8/89).

The public in Finland has just recently become aware of the foreign military sales issue. There are several reasons for this. First, the only thorough study of Finnish foreign military sales to date was published in 1984 (Huru et al. 1984). Second, public opinion was influenced by information and debates in Sweden during the 1980s. Third, Finnish companies have recently been noted for their involvement in alleged illegal sales. According to a public opinion poll in May of 1988, close to 50 per cent of the population wanted Finland's foreign military sales to stop (*Hufvudstadsbladet*, May 24, 1988).

It has been suggested in Finland that control requirements similar to some of the more recent Swedish requirements should be introduced (*Report of the party working on war materiel export* 1988). Paradoxically, among the reasons mentioned for new requirements, which are supported by Finland's Defense Minister, is that more up-to-date

FIGURE 4.1
Foreign military sales in million constant (1985) U.S.$ *

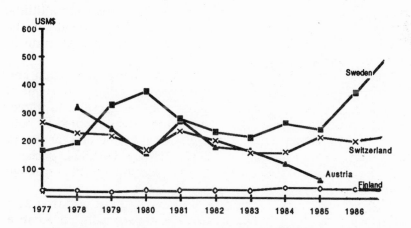

* The trends have been calculated by the author on the basis of data supplied from the different countries (see Appendix tables). Annual averages of the dollar exchange rate have been used. For the Swiss trend for the period 1977 to 1984, see also Brzoska and Ohlson (1987, p. 109).

requirements are necessary in order to control *increasing* foreign military sales (*Hufvudstadsbladet*, January 8, 1988). This leads us to the question of the implementation of formal policy.

4.2   ACTUAL POLICY

Value of Foreign Military Sales Over Time

Figure 4.1 illustrates the development of actual neutral war materiel sales in constant dollars during the period 1977-1987 according to national sources. Other sources may give different results. For instance, ACDA figures (in constant 1984 U.S.$) contain some important deviations from figure 4.1 (*World Military Expenditures and Arms Transfers* 1987, table II). The ACDA trend for Switzerland is more or less a constant decrease since 1977 from a value of more than $700 million worth of foreign military sales. The Austrian trend according to ACDA includes increases in 1978 and 1981 but also depicts increases in 1983, 1984 and 1986. The value for Finland's foreign military sales is also low according to ACDA figures but shows important peaks in 1979 and 1983-1984. During the latter peak, the ACDA value of Finnish sales was higher than the sum of sales from Austria and Sweden. According to ACDA, Sweden experienced drastic reductions in foreign sales in 1983 and in 1986.

There are thus important differences between ACDA trends and those calculated from national statistics. Such differences also occur for other nations (see Kolodziej 1979 for a comparison with French figures). The difference in exchange rates between 1984 (the ACDA base year) and 1985 (the base year used in figure 4.1) cannot explain these differences. The main explanation lies in which types of information are compiled and how they are interpreted by ACDA. Its figures represent (*World Military Expenditures and Arms Transfers* 1986, p. 158)

'the international transfer (under terms of grant, credit, barter or cash) of military equipment, usually referred to as 'conventional', including weapons of war, parts thereof, ammunition, support equipment, and other commodities designed for military use. – Dual use equipment is included when its primary mission is identified as military. The building of defense production facilities and licensing fees paid as royalties for the production of military equipment are included when they are contained in military transfer agreements. – Excluded are foodstuffs, medical equipment, petroleum products, and other supplies. Military services such as construction, training, and technical support are not included for the United States, whose services consist mainly of construction. Military services of other countries, which are normally of a much smaller magnitude, are included'.

It is clear that ACDA includes more than do the neutrals in their definitions of war materiel. Examples are dual-use equipment and licensing fees. This should result in higher ACDA figures than those in neutral statistics. No such general difference is obvious from the preceding comparison. This does explain, however, the two peaks in ACDA figures for Finland, which included sales of dual-use ships to the Soviet Union. The same type of explanation might be true for the peaks in Austrian sales, although this has not been possible to verify.

ACDA statistics are collected by different U.S. government sources, mainly the Defense Intelligence Agency (Brzoska 1982, p. 91). The data can be assumed to include whatever information is available (*World Military Expenditures and Arms Transfers* 1986, p. 159):

'Figures for the United States are obtained from official trade statistics on military transfers compiled by the US Department of Defense and State. – The US data include commercial deliveries of items some of which may be intended for civilian rather than military use.

Data on countries other than the United States are estimates by United States Government sources. Arms transfer data for the Soviet Union and other communist countries are approximations based on limited information'.

This would include official as well as unofficial information, public as well as classified, originating from suppliers as well as recipients. The supply of information ought therefore to be impressive. The important question is how this mass of information is compiled, analyzed and presented. Of this we know nothing because ACDA does not publish detailed information about its sources (for further discussion of quantitative problems, see Blackaby & Ohlson 1982; Brzoska 1982).

Due to the insecurities surrounding ACDA estimates of neutral foreign military sales, the national figures have been used. Official national statistics are available for three of the four neutrals. Austrian foreign military sales have been estimated for the larger part of the period 1977-1987 using annual company reports. Nevertheless, this is an unfortunate situation because ACDA is the only organization that regularly publishes international data of this type. Given that some countries do not publish *any* national military statistics, ACDA would be more valuable for research purposes if it were more explicit with regard to its sources and their validity and if it related its findings to available national statistics.

The special position of Finland is immediately recognized in figure 4.1. The value of foreign military sales has been low and almost constant since 1977. There were no sales of important materiel to Third World countries between 1971 and 1985 (Brzoska & Ohlson 1987, p. 106). The foreign military sales shadow is not very visible. This result is congruent with the Domestic Policy Tool outcome and is supported by the finding in Chapter 3 that relatively strong support exists for Finland's domestic market. An additional and supporting explanation may be the peace treaty prohibitions of producing war materiel in excess of the needs of the armed forces. In the case of Finland, therefore, there is reason to assume that the trend reflects relatively few attempts to sell military supplies abroad rather than a failure to meet international demands. This also supports the finding that the foreign military sales issue has not until recently raised the interest and concern of the general public.

While Finland shows the most continuous trend, Austria shows the most irregular. There was no military production in Austria until the State Treaty in 1955. Moreover, up to the 1970s, Austrian foreign military sales were confined mainly to small arms and ammunition. The extended production of Steyer-Daimler-Puch and Voest-Alpine around that time was mainly for foreign customers. This is illustrated by the high proportion of production devoted to foreign sales between 1979 and 1982 (table 4.2). No other neutral shows a foreign military sales share of total military production greater than 50 per cent. This is also illustrated by the export peaks in 1977 and 1981 in figure 4.1.

Austrian developments fit the Business as Usual as well as the Domestic Policy Tool outcome. The figures indicate a willingness on the part of the Austrian government to accept major production for foreign customers. Austrian military production, however, has been too narrow to be competitive on the international market. The decline in Third World orders during the 1980s (*World Armaments and Disarmament* 1985, 1986) caused a reduction, or even the disappearance, of many Austrian foreign markets. Recent estimates suggest that the value of foreign military sales has remained around the 1985 level (*Milavnews*, Austria, AAS-8/89). This helps explain why Austria has failed to acquired an armament rhythm.

TABLE 4.2
Foreign military sales: Share of domestic military production (%)

	1977	1978	1979	1980	1981	1982	1983	1984	1985
Austria	55	70	71	73	92	68	38	11	-
Finland	38	43	29	31	33	31	28	35	31
Sweden	16	18	27	30	25	22	21	26	22
Switzerland	44	37	36	30	35	36	32	19	22

Since the late 1970s Sweden has moved from being among the smallest neutral suppliers to being the largest. There were important increases in the value of Swedish foreign military sales in 1978-1979 and from 1985 on. Rather than demonstrating Restraint, Sweden has come to represent the Legitimization outcome. The decrease in the defense share of GNP/GDP in Sweden has been parallelled by increasing foreign military sales. Despite several setbacks, Sweden has been relatively successful on the international market due to the nation's relatively broad military production. This finding most clearly illustrates the gap between formal policy and implementation; even with the most restrictive formal policy – with new control requirements coming into effect as late as 1983 – Sweden shows the highest values of foreign military sales.

The 1978 change in the Swiss attitude toward a loose implementation of policy has not resulted in any major increase in the value of total foreign military sales. Switzerland's curve reflects, on the whole, a relatively constant value of total sales with only slight increases in 1981 and 1985. Nevertheless, the value of Switzerland's military sales between 1981 and 1985 was of roughly the same magnitude as were sales from Sweden during the same period. These findings correspond with the indicators presented in Chapter 3. The relatively large military industrial base and the relatively advanced military production in both Sweden and Switzerland are reflected by their relatively high values of foreign military sales.

Only Finland so far seems to fit the postulated results. Sweden is a country clearly indicating a loose implementation of formal policy. What has mainly determined the Austrian trend seems to be variations in international demands. It should be noted, however, that the values are quite low in comparison with the world's largest military suppliers. As a result, one or two major foreign military deals may have important effects upon the foreign military sales trend. This explains the roughly equal values of foreign military sales from Austria and Switzerland between 1979 and 1983 when Austrian sales

TABLE 4.3
Foreign Swedish military sales: Regional distribution*

| Recipient | % of Total Sales | | | |
Region	1971-1975	1976-1980	1981-1985	1986-1987
Americas	4.5	5.9	10.5	15.2
North A.	2.3	2.3	5.7	9.6
Central A.	0.0	0.0	0.6	0.5
South A.	2.2	3.6	4.2	5.1
Europe	79.1	60.6	52.3	46.5
NATO E.	42.5	35.2	32.7	26.1
WTO incl. USSR	0.0	0.2	0.0	0.0
Other E.	36.6	25.2	19.6	20.4
Middle East	1.0	1.4	0.0	0.0
Africa	1.5	4.4	8.1	1.1
Northwest A.	0.0	0.0	0.0	0.0
East A.	0.0	0.0	0.0	0.0
Southern A.	0.0	0.0	0.0	0.0
Other A.	1.5	4.4	8.1	1.1
Asia	13.8	27.8	29.1	37.2
South A.	8.1	4.1	5.8	28.2
Southeast A.	5.2	22.8	20.0	7.3
Other A. incl A/NZ	0.5	0.9	3.3	1.7

TABLE 4.3, continued

	Average No. of Recipients/Year			
	1971-1975	1976-1980	1981-1985	1986-1987
	6.0	6.2	5.8	6.5
	2.0	2.0	2.0	2.0
	0.0	0.4	0.6	0.5
	4.0	3.8	3.2	4.0
	17.6	20.4	21.6	19.5
	11.4	11.2	12.8	12.0
	1.2	3.2	3.0	2.5
	5.0	6.0	5.8	5.0
	0.8	1.0	0.0	0.0
	0.8	2.2	2.8	3.0
	0.2	0.2	0.0	0.0
	0.0	0.0	0.0	0.0
	0.2	0.0	0.0	0.0
	0.4	2.0	2.8	3.0
	9.0	9.4	10.4	10.0
	2.0	2.0	2.6	3.0
	3.6	3.6	3.2	3.0
	3.4	3.8	4.6	4.0
Total average no. of recipients/year	34.2	39.2	40.6	39.0

* Based on data in Appendix B.

TABLE 4.4
Foreign Swiss military sales: Regional distribution*

Recipient Region	% of Total Sales			
	1971-1975	1976-1980	1981-1985	1986-1987
Americas	4.5	3.0	3.6	7.3
North A.	0.8	0.9	2.2	4.8
Central A.	0.4	0.0	0.0	0.0
South A.	3.3	2.1	1.4	2.5
Europe	55.1	84.2	67.7	54.1
NATO E.	43.4	68.5	50.0	43.7
WTO incl. USSR	0.0	0.0	0.0	0.0
Other E.	11.7	15.7	17.7	10.4
Middle East	34.5	6.5	8.8	22.9
Africa	0.3	3.9	17.3	8.0
Northwest A.	0.1	0.4	0.5	0.4
East A.	0.0	0.0	0.0	0.0
Southern A.	0.0	0.0	0.0	0.0
Other A.	0.2	3.5	16.8	7.6
Asia	5.5	2.4	2.6	7.7
South A.	0.0	0.0	0.0	3.4
Southeast A.	3.1	2.0	1.9	4.0
Other A. incl A/NZ	2.4	0.4	0.7	0.3
Other	0.1	0.1	0.0	0.0

TABLE 4.4, continued

| | Average No. of Recipients/Year | | | |
	1971-1975	1976-1980	1981-1985	1986-1987
	5.6	6.8	7.6	8.0
	1.8	2.0	2.0	2.0
	0.4	0.2	0.4	0.0
	3.4	4.6	5.2	6.0
	14.4	15.2	16.0	16.0
	11.0	11.2	12.0	12.0
	0.0	0.0	0.0	0.0
	3.4	4.0	4.0	4.0
	1.0	1.4	4.4	4.5
	1.0	3.8	4.6	6.0
	0.8	2.0	2.0	2.0
	0.0	0.0	0.0	0.0
	0.0	0.2	1.0	1.0
	0.2	1.6	1.6	3.0
	3.2	5.0	8.0	9.0
	0.0	0.2	1.6	2.0
	2.0	3.6	4.4	5.5
	1.2	1.2	2.0	1.5
	-	-	-	-
Total average no. of recipients/year	25.2	32.2	40.6	43.5

* Based on data in Appendix C.

TABLE 4.5
Foreign Finnish military sales: Regional distribution*

Recipient Region	% of Total Sales			
	1971-1975	1976-1980	1981-1985	1986-1987
Americas	28.4	12.5	14.1	20.7
North A.	27.4	10.7	12.5	19.4
Central A.	0.2	0.3	0.2	0.0
South A.	0.7	1.4	1.3	1.3
Europe	55.4	68.8	59.4	71.6
NATO E.	32.4	36.5	34.7	42.4
WTO incl. USSR	0.6	1.8	1.7	5.2
Other E.	22.5	30.6	23.0	24.0
Middle East	1.2	5.4	1.2	0.4
Africa	0.2	0.1	1.0	0.1
Northwest A.	0.1	0.0	0.0	0.0
East A.	0.0	0.0	0.8	0.0
Southern A.	0.0	0.0	0.1	0.0
Other A.	0.1	0.1	0.1	0.1
Asia	14.8	13.2	24.4	7.2
South A.	0.0	0.0	0.0	0.0
Southeast A.	9.9	7.9	21.0	4.4
Other A. incl A/NZ	4.9	5.4	3.4	2.8
Other	0.0	0.0	0.0	0.0

TABLE 4.5, continued

	Average No. of Recipients/Year			
	1971-1975	1976-1980	1981-1985	1986-1987
	7.4	6.8	7.6	9.0
	2.0	2.0	2.0	2.0
	2.4	1.0	0.8	0.5
	3.0	3.8	4.8	6.5
	22.2	21.2	22.0	23.5
	11.0	12.0	12.4	13.0
	5.4	3.4	4.2	5.0
	5.8	5.8	5.4	5.5
	3.2	2.6	3.8	2.5
	2.4	0.4	2.8	4.0
	0.2	0.0	0.0	0.5
	0.2	0.0	0.2	0.0
	1.0	0.0	1.2	1.5
	1.0	0.4	1.4	2.0
	6.0	6.6	8.4	10.5
	0.4	0.0	0.4	1.0
	3.2	4.0	4.2	3.5
	2.4	2.6	3.8	6.0
	-	-	-	-
Total average no. of recipients/year	41.2	37.6	44.6	49.5

* Based on data in Appendix A.

were at their peak. Sales of howitzers to India likewise explain the sharp increase in Sweden's sales after 1985.

With regard to Switzerland it is at this stage difficult to clearly define the outcome. The reason is that it is not yet possible to distinguish between attempted, but failed, foreign military sales, on the one hand, and a lack of effort to sell, on the other. As we continue the analysis, however, the Swiss outcome will become clear.

Number of Recipients

The regions in tables 4.3-4.5 have been defined on the basis of European military-political groupings (alliances) and broad zones of conflict. As was suggested previously, neutral nations should not make foreign military sales to only one of the major European alliances. Neutrals should also exercise restraint in military sales to conflict zones and to nations involved in armed conflict.

The following analysis is a general test of these conditions. It will not deal with domestic conflicts or with the supression of human rights. In order to understand the results the reader should know how the recipients have been grouped (see Appendix D). It should be noted that Spain has been grouped with NATO for the whole period. Egypt, Iran and Iraq have been included in the Middle East. The Caribbean and West Indian islands, except Trinidad and Tobago, are listed as part of Central America.

Tables 4.3-4.5 show the regional distribution of sales from Sweden, Switzerland and Finland, respectively. Because there are no detailed figures of foreign military sales from Austria, it has been left out of the following analysis. The tables have been organized in five-year periods, with the exception of 1986-1987. For each period the percentage of regional shares and the number of recipients have been calculated. In this chapter we will concentrate upon the *number* of recipients. In the following chapter, recipients will be analyzed with regard to their *economic shares*.

In total: All recipients listed in the original national compilations have been included in the analysis. The total number of recipients today is surprisingly similar at an average of forty customers per year. This represents 25 per cent of all nations.

During the early 1970s, Switzerland had an average number of twenty-five recipients per year, the lowest number for all the neutrals. Sweden had an average of thirty-four recipients per year. At that time Finland already had about forty customers.

For the whole period, Switzerland's global market has increased the most rapidly. None of the neutrals seems to have attempted to keep a low and constant, not to mention reduced, number of recipients. Finland again shows the most stable trend, albeit with a relatively large number of recipients and a constant increase from 1976. With regard to the total number of recipients, the implementation of formal policy can therefore be defined as loose in all countries.

By military alliance and region. The neutrals sell military materiel to members of the European military alliances. Most of the neutrals reflect an unbalanced choice of customers between East and West. Their recipients are predominantly found in Western Europe, and the majority of European customers are NATO members. In addition to the European NATO members, the United States and Canada also receive war materiel from the neutrals. Because Switzerland makes no military sales to Eastern European countries, Switzerland has the most pronounced Western bias of all the neutrals.

Only Finland comes close to equally dividing its recipients between East and West. Finland's special relationship with the Soviet Union has permitted a military market in the Soviet Union and Eastern Europe. The number of recipients in Eastern Europe is almost equal to that in the 'other Europe'.

The number of recipients in Latin America has increased for both Finland and Switzerland. Both also have customers in the Middle East. For Sweden, the Middle East has been a very small legal military market, and it gradually diminished during the 1980s. This is in sharp contrast to Switzerland, for which there has been a constant increase of recipients in that region.

With the exception of 1986 and 1987, Africa has been the smallest military market for Finland in terms of number of recipients. Sweden and especially Switzerland have both continually increased their number of recipients in Africa. Since 1986, most African recipients of war materiel from Switzerland and Finland have been located in southern Africa. There have been no Swedish recipients in southern Africa since the middle of the 1970s.

Asia has been the second largest neutral military market during the entire period. The number of Asian recipients has steadily increased. For Switzerland, the number of Asian customers has more than doubled since the early 1970s.

In summary, although there are some signs of restraint, the general and most important conclusion is that with regard to numbers of recipients, the neutrals reflect a loose implementation of formal policy. There has been an increase in the number of customers for all three countries since 1976. All of the neutrals show a Western bias in their foreign military sales. Both Finland and Switzerland have customers in some of the most pronounced zones of international conflict, such as southern Africa and the Middle East. In contrast there are no Swedish recipients today in these zones of conflict. Appendix D shows that Finland is more visible than any of the other neutrals in Central America, the Middle East, the Far East and southern Africa.

As is evident from the appendices, the list of recipients from Finland and Switzerland contain a group of undefined recipients. The total number of recipients from Finland and Switzerland should thus be slightly higher. Alternatively, some Swedish recipients should be excluded. This means that the number of recipients in tables 4.4 and 4.5, at least for some regions, should be higher. Because the number of recipients in some regions is quite small, the influence of one or two additional recipients can in those regions be important.

The magnitude of this inconsistency is reduced when the economic shares are compared. The reason is that the 'other' countries can be assumed to be relatively small recipients with only a minor impact upon the total economic shares. In some known Swedish and Swiss cases, such smaller sales consisted of arms and ammunition for hunting and target practice.

According to Shares

Value of regional/alliance and major recipient shares. The decline in Third World markets which had such drastic results for Austria has not been as severe for the other neutrals. The reason is that they have not been as heavily dependent upon sales of armored vehicles or upon sales to Third World recipients. The European market accounts for 50 per cent or more of total military sales from Finland, Sweden and Switzerland. NATO accounts for more than 40 per cent of sales from Finland and Switzerland. Only Sweden has decreased its percentage of total military sales to Europe and NATO. The turning point occurred in 1984 when, according to the War Materiel Inspectorate, the total Western European share of Swedish war materiel exports was 50 per cent. This should be compared to more than 80 per cent during individual years in the early 1970s. For Finland, Sweden and Switzerland, Western industrialized recipients (roughly one-third of all the recipients) account for the largest share of total military sales.

It has been suggested that 5 per cent or more reflect important political interaction between seller and buyer (Wallensteen 1973, p. 67). Figure 4.2 shows the war materiel recipients which accounted for

5 per cent or more of total military sales from the neutrals during the period from 1971 to 1987. The nine major recipients of war materiel from Sweden accounted for a little more than 60 per cent of total Swedish foreign military sales during that period. Six of the major recipients were Western European countries. All recipients went down one step on the ranking ladder in 1986 due to Swedish deliveries of howitzers to India.

The seven major recipients of war materiel from Switzerland accounted for more than 65 per cent of total Swiss foreign military sales. The most important recipient, the Federal Republic of Germany, accounted for more than 20 per cent of total sales. This was the largest share of any individual recipient. Sweden was at the bottom of the Swiss list. Non-European recipients accounted for relatively high shares of total foreign military sales from Switzerland.

Finland's war materiel sales were strongly oriented toward a few large recipients. The five major recipients together accounted for 55 per cent of total military sales. It should be noted that Sweden was the major foreign recipient. The third largest recipient (Singapore) was the only non-European recipient.

It was noted previously that the number of recipients of war materiel from Finland in Eastern Europe is about the same as in the 'other Europe'. The value of sales and the relative shares of these recipients are much lower, however. Finland thereby resembles the other neutrals in their bias toward Western European recipients. This should come as no major surprise, as there really is no military market for Western military supplies in the Soviet Union and Eastern European countries.

From tables 4.3-4.5 the Third World shares can be calculated by adding the percentages of total sales to the Middle East, Central and South America, Africa and Asia. The Third World share has constantly increased for each of the three neutrals since the middle of the 1970s. For Finland, the Third World market is still relatively small, however – only around 25 per cent of total war materiel sales. For Switzerland, there was a decrease following a high of 40 per cent in the early 1970s, mainly due to a sharp decrease in Middle Eastern sales. The share is slowly approaching the former high due to sales to Africa (1981-1985) and the Middle East (1986-1987). Swedish sales to the Third World have constantly increased, mainly due to increasing sales to Asia. These figures are consistent with the SIPRI finding that Sweden and Switzerland have been the only neutrals among the fifteen major suppliers of important materiel to Third World countries since the early 1960s (*World Armaments and Disarmament* 1978, 1986).

FIGURE 4.2
Foreign military sales: Major Finnish, Swedish and Swiss recipients
and shares, 1971-1987 (5 % or more of total sales)*

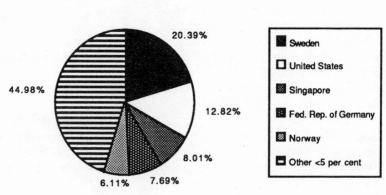

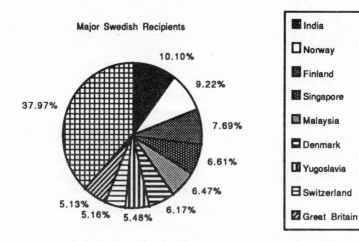

FIGURE 4.2, continued

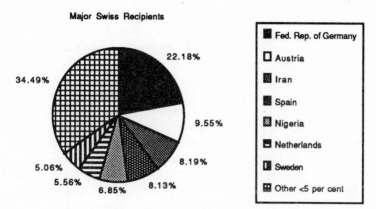

Major Swiss Recipients

* Based on data in Appendix tables A-C.

The explicit political decision in Switzerland of a loose implementation of formal policy explains why recipients can be found in the Middle East and southern Africa despite control requirements excluding zones of conflict. Recipients such as Dubai, Bahrain and Saudi Arabia more than counterbalance the loss of Iran as a major Middle Eastern recipient in 1978 (see also Appendix C).

For Sweden, the picture is different. The statistics reflect a tendency to stay away from the main zones of conflict, such as Central America, the Middle East and southern Africa. Apart from Iran, which was a Swedish recipient until 1981, no country in the Middle East has officially and directly received Swedish war materiel.

In summary, the Western export orientation has been further emphasized by the preceding analysis. Finland's customers in Eastern Europe are of little economic importance. Despite an increasing relative importance, the Third World does not account for more than 50 per cent of sales from any of the neutrals.

Finland and Switzerland show no inclination to embargo direct sales to zones of military conflict. Instead, it seems as if they are taking advantage of zones of conflict in their attempts to sell military supplies. Military sales from Switzerland to the Middle East and southern Africa are becoming proportionately more important over time.

For all of the neutrals, the major recipients account for more than 50 per cent of total military sales. Although the number of major recipients is low (between five and nine), they support the pattern that we have already seen: Sweden, the major neutral military producer, has the highest number of major recipients, followed by Switzerland and Finland, respectively.

Again we make a surprising finding with regard to Finland's military sales. The U.S. market has generally been difficult to enter due to U.S. protective measures. It is therefore surprising to note that North America (the United States and Canada) has accounted for more than 10 per cent of total Finnish war materiel sales. During the early 1970s, the share was more than 25 per cent and is today close to 20 per cent. Most of this share is accounted for by the United States.

Why is this? Two reasons may be suggested. First, Finnish foreign military sales are mainly composed of powder, ammunition and light arms for which there is a rather large global market. This may also explain the increase in foreign recipients since 1976. The Buy American Act is probably not as strictly applied to these types of supplies as to supplies that compete with important U.S. materiel.

But if this is true for sales from Finland, why is it not also true of sales from the other neutrals given that they all produce these kinds of supplies? A second possible reason could therefore be, as with the training of Finnish officers in the United States (Hagelin 1986), that U.S. purchases of war materiel from Finland are a way of supporting Finland's military production and defense without the United States being clearly visible. Should U.S. support take other, more visible forms, it might create difficulties for Finland's foreign policy vis-à-vis the Soviet Union.

We conclude this part with a more detailed analysis of the neutrals as recipients. Have the neutrals, in order to maximize the credibility of their neutral policies, directed their military trade toward the other neutrals?

Value of neutral recipients. In table 4.6, Swedish annual sales to the other neutrals have been compiled. The total figures are greater than 5 per cent for all years but one, which indicates that the neutrals as a group have been of some importance. During the 1980s, however, the share decreased and varied more than before.

As individual recipients, the other neutral countries are not major recipients of Swedish war materiel. This is confirmed by figure 4.2. Finland ranks third and Switzerland as number eight. Austria does not show up at all in table 4.6. The figures for each individual recipient country are generally low and varying. The few high figures in sales to

TABLE 4.6
Neutral shares of Swedish war materiel sales, 1971-1987 (%)*

Recipient	1971	1972	1973	1974	1975	1976	1977	1978	1979	1980	1981	1982	1983	1984	1985	1986	1987
Austria	15	18	2	1	3	4	6	2	1	2	3	3	3	4	1	2	8
Finland	<1	5	28	31	13	7	7	4	2	2	3	3	3	5	16	16	7
Switzerland	13	14	10	7	12	9	12	12	2	7	10	9	5	1	3	3	2
Total	28	37	40	39	28	20	25	18	5	11	16	15	11	9	20	21	17

TABLE 4.7
Neutral shares of Finnish war materiel sales, 1971-1987 (%)*

Recipient	1971	1972	1973	1974	1975	1976	1977	1978	1979	1980	1981	1982	1983	1984	1985	1986	1987
Austria	2	2	2	3	3	2	2	2	2	1	4	2	2	3	3	4	3
Sweden	25	18	14	14	25	28	29	21	29	29	24	19	18	16	16	18	17
Switzerland	<1	<1	<1	<1	1	<1	1	1	1	1	3	2	2	1	1	1	1
Total	27	20	16	17	29	30	32	24	32	31	31	23	22	20	20	23	21

TABLE 4.8
Neutral shares of Swiss war materiel sales, 1971-1987 (%)*

Recipient	1971	1972	1973	1974	1975	1976	1977	1978	1979	1980	1981	1982	1983	1984	1985	1986	1987
Austria	3	4	9	32	3	8	9	9	16	7	15	14	19	7	3	4	7
Finland	<1	<1	<1	<1	<1	<1	<1	<1	<1	1	<1	<1	<1	<1	<1	<1	<1
Sweden	3	3	2	2	2	2	3	5	6	15	9	8	6	5	3	4	5
Total	6	7	11	34	5	10	12	14	22	23	24	22	25	12	6	8	12

* Based on data in Appendix tables A-C.

Austria during the early 1970s can be explained by the sale of Swedish aircraft. Aircraft and aircraft parts have also been a major category of goods sold to Finland, which explains the high figures during the 1970s. The increases in 1985 and 1986 are explained by the sale of guided missiles.

In contrast, the high figures for sales to Switzerland reflect a more varied trade. Switzerland is the only neutral recipient which exceeds 5 per cent of total Swedish foreign military sales for most of the studied period. Thus, despite Finland's higher ranking in figure 4.2, Switzerland has been a more stable recipient. During most of the 1980s, however, Switzerland accounted for less than 5 per cent.

Apart from guided missiles, Sweden during the 1970s and 1980s sold very few important military supplies abroad. There are no foreign customers for Swedish battle tanks. The first and so far only foreign order for Swedish submarines was signed recently with Australia. Only a few major surface ships and fighter aircraft have been sold. It is therefore all the more interesting to note that with the exception of sales to Denmark, all fighter aircraft have been supplied to neutral countries. Austria is the largest customer with more than one hundred Swedish aircraft bought since the 1950s, including non-jet trainers (*Svenska Dagbladet*, February 16, 1986). About forty of the jet trainer/light attack aircraft Saab 105 and twenty of the jet fighter aircraft 'Flygande Tunnan' ('the Flying Barrel') have been sold to Austria. Saab 105s have been delivered since 1970. Draken fighters were sold to Finland as well as to Austria (and to Denmark) during the 1970s. These sales are clearly reflected in table 4.6. Swedish aircraft make up roughly one-half of Austria's and Finland's military aircraft inventory. In that respect Sweden has been a more important supplier than the statistics indicate.

As already noted, Finnish foreign military sales are strongly oriented toward a few major recipients. Neither Austria nor Switzerland is among the major recipients. Sweden is Finland's major military customer. Sweden has been a stable recipient of Finnish war materiel – more stable than either Finland or Switzerland as recipients of Swedish war materiel (table 4.7). While Finland accounted for almost 8 per cent of Sweden's foreign military sales between 1971 and 1987, Sweden accounted for more than 20 per cent of Finnish military sales during the same period (figure 4.2).

There are very few neutrals among the seven major recipients of war materiel from Switzerland. The major neutral recipient is Austria. Sweden barely exceeded 5 per cent of Swiss sales except between 1978 and 1984 and again in 1987. The most exceptional year was 1980, when Sweden was the major neutral military recipient of war materiel from Switzerland. The neutrals as a group increased their share of Swiss military sales from around 5 per cent in 1975 to between 22 and 25 per cent between 1979 and 1983 (table 4.8). A change occurred in 1985, however, when Third World recipients became relatively more important in Swiss foreign military sales. This caused a reduction in the share of neutral recipients to the levels of the early 1970s.

Does Neutrality Matter?

Can the exceptional Swedish aircraft sales be explained by neutrality? Would not the neutrals, just as NATO members, feel a desire to buy from each other? Alas, such a common policy denominator seems insufficient in explaining these sales. If neutral policy was such an important factor, the figures for Swedish as well as Finnish and Swiss military sales to the other neutrals should be higher.

It is not possible, without access to the minutes from the negotiations, to definitely conclude that neutrality was of *no* importance. General information seems to indicate, however, that the financial content of international agreements has, with increasing international competition, in general become more and more important (Brzoska & Ohlson 1987) – at least as important a criterion as the foreign policy of the supplier. There is no indication that this should be different for neutral countries. For the paying government, the military requirements should be fulfilled at as low a price as possible. This can be achieved through offsets.

Offsets might perpetuate uncompetitive practices. As stated by Leo Welt, the then President of a U.S. trading company (Welt 1984, p. 25): 'Many countries use countertrade to market products of inferior quality or products that are otherwise uncompetitive in the international market. In other words, it is a way of unloading otherwise unmarketable goods'.

Despite Welt's opposition to offsets as a general trading practice, his point seems correct in the Swedish case. All of the Swedish fighter aircraft sold were surplus. Although they were relatively cheap, it was difficult to find interested customers because there were younger/better aircraft available on the international market. To make them desirable, offsets became important. It might be that offsets were easier to arrange with neutrals than with other customers. It could also be that better offsets were offered to neutrals than to other potential customers. If so, the neutral policies had an important economic consequence. But there is nothing in the material presented here to support the argument that policy was able to compensate for economic realities and technological demands.

Offsets aim to reduce or compensate for the cost of military purchases. They can take different forms, but they have two things in common. First, they are commercial means of competition. Second, they involve mainly bilateral trade. When nation A imports military supplies from supplier B, the latter agrees to compensate nation A by purchasing supplies from or creating jobs in nation A. When Finland ordered the first J35 'Draken' package in 1970, Saab-Scania promised offsets worth roughly 40 per cent of the total value of the contract. The package included manufacture of rivetted components for the aircraft, such as frames, landing gear gates, rear wing ends and air intakes. Valmet also became a major car subcontractor to Saab-Scania in Sweden. The offsets were fulfilled before the expiration of the contract (*Samhällsekonomisk analys* 1976, pp. 59-60; Harle 1977).

The Finnish contract for more Draken aircraft in 1984, as well as the purchase of the Saab anti-ship missile rb-15, also included compensations. This time the compensations accounted for more than 100 per cent of the cost of the aircraft (*Upsala Nya Tidning*, November 12, 1986). Saab was in charge of the offsets, which consisted mainly of deliveries to the Saab car division in Sweden (*Tempus*, April 18, 1984; *Flight International*, March 12, 1983, p. 634).

In Austria, offsets were included in the Saab 105 jet trainer deal and were fulfilled ahead of schedule (*International Defence Review* 1976, no. 3, p. 489). After many years of negotiation, it has been said that complete (100 per cent) offsets were also a major factor in concluding the Austrian Draken deal in 1985 (*International Defence Review* 1984, no. 11, p. 1602). Even before the deal had been concluded, Saab had ordered car parts as well as ammunition in Austria. Saab promised that at least 30 per cent of the compensations would be in the form of technology transfer. A factory in Austria to manufacture aircraft parts was planned, and an administrative office was opened in Vienna.

That aircraft deal caused a major stir in Austria. The public critique against the deal focused mainly on two aspects: that the aircraft was outdated – and therefore an unnecessary expenditure – and that it was noisy. There were also accusations that Austria paid an overprice for the aircraft as well as allegations of bribes. The Austrian government, however, was not prepared to go back on the deal. Instead, the flight training was transferred to the Vidsel military proving ground in northern Sweden instead of taking place in Austria. The first aircraft were delivered in June of 1988 and the last in May of 1989. A probable explanation of the Austrian government's reluctance to accept the critique is the option to negotiate a favorable purchasing price for the new Swedish JAS39 'Gripen' aircraft (*Dagens Industri*, April 12, 15 and 16, 1985; *Dagens Nyheter*, May 22, 1985; *Flight International*, June 1, 1985).

Thus, under very special circumstances neutrality may be a commercial advantage. One explicit illustration is the recent Austrian order for Swedish 'Bill' anti-tank missiles. A representative of the Austrian Ministry of Defense stated that because the tests showed virtually no important differences between the 'Bill' and the 'Milan 2', Swedish neutrality tipped the balance to the advantage of 'Bill' (*Svenska Dagbladet*, June 16, 1989)[1].

Under normal conditions, however, neutral recipients are not as important as the major non-neutral recipients are. The former pass the 5 per cent mark mostly as a result of extraordinary sales rather than as a result of long-term trends. Sweden is the only neutral which ranks as the number one customer of another neutral. Its share of Finland's foreign military sales is equal to the share of the Federal Republic of Germany in Switzerland's military sales. This Swedish position also reflects other findings. Sweden has moved toward outcome B. Although Sweden has not mainly produced military materiel for foreign customers and has refrained from direct military sales to traditional zones of military conflict, Sweden has shown no restraint with regard to other indicators. There has been an increase in both the value of total foreign military sales and in the number of recipients. Sweden has also shown a strong Western bias in both the number and value of its military sales.

The curve representing the value of total Swiss foreign military sales has been relatively stable. Military production has not primarily been for foreign customers. Other indicators, however, such as the number of recipients, the Western export orientation and the value of military sales to zones of conflict, reflect outcome D. Switzerland is the only neutral where the neutral dilemma has been 'solved' by a formal political decision.

The stable value of Finland's total foreign military sales over time and the existence of customers in both East and West may lead one to believe that Finland has had a strict implementation of formal policy (outcome C). But with regard to the high and increasing number of recipients, the low share of military sales to Eastern Europe, the relatively high share of the United States in total foreign military sales and the value of military sales to regions of conflict, Finland has moved toward outcome D.

Austria is the only neutral which for a period produced military materiel mainly for foreign customers. The reduction in the value of total Austrian military sales seems to have been determined by international competition. As noted, the statistical data for Austria do not permit any more detailed analysis of Austrian foreign military sales.

War materiel sales have been guided primarily by *proximity*, except in some odd years for individual countries. Finland's major neutral market is Sweden, Sweden's major neutral market is Finland, and Switzerland's major neutral market is Austria. Available data indicate that trade is one-way or at least unbalanced (in percentage terms). It is also worth noting that – accounting for the gap in Austrian information – apart from the Federal Republic of Germany, Norway and Singapore, no major non-neutral recipients show up on the major recipients list of more than one neutral country.

A logical explanation would be that it is easier to trade the closer the distance between the supplier and the recipient. But in today's world with daily, easy and quick international communications, this would seem an insufficient explanation. If a short distance was such an important factor, how would one explain sales to, for instance, India or Singapore?

It is suggested here that other than geographical factors explain the proximity result. The most obvious, especially with regard to Sweden and Finland, are *historical* factors. Sweden and Finland were until 1809 one country. Other explanations, which fit well also Switzerland and Austria, are *linguistic* and *cultural*. Trade is easier to achieve when one can easily communicate orally and in writing and when one understand the other's habits and customs. Sweden was for a long time a major European power, and the Swedish influence upon Finnish culture in particular was strong. Swedish was, and still is, the native language for groups and individuals in Finland. In Austrian and Swiss history, Germany has been the major power, and German is a language spoken in both countries.

Such historical, linguistic and cultural similarities have of course been possible due to geographical proximity. But they are probably more important than the geographical closeness as such. These factors are, of course, of no importance if there is nothing to be traded, if there is a lack of demand in the other country or if there are political differences. Proximity, however, helps create similar military demands due to similar geography. Sweden and Finland are both in the same climatic region, and both have mountainous and flat regions broken up by rivers and lakes. Both countries are situated by the Baltic Sea.

A similar conclusion can be drawn for Austria and Switzerland. They are situated in the same part of Europe. Both are mountainous.

None has any demand for a Navy. Treaty restrictions upon Austria, however, reduce the sphere of similar demands between the two countries to a larger extent than is the case between Sweden and Finland.

What, then, determines the *direction* of trade? A plausible assumption would be that the country with the largest military industrial base would supply the state with a relatively smaller industrial base. This is confirmed by trade between Sweden and Finland and between Sweden and Switzerland. The fact that Austria has been a more important market to Finland than has Switzerland also fits this conclusion. Due to lack of information, it is not possible to draw any definite conclusions about the relationship between Austria and Switzerland.

The quantitative data are not, however, as convincing with regard to trade between Sweden and Switzerland as between Sweden and Finland. A complementary explanation suggested here is that the more equal the trading partners are with regard to military industrial base and production, the more important are particular demands in each country in defining the direction of trade. This is illustrated by the exchange between Sweden and Switzerland of military supplies, including R&D. This cooperation is more of a 'give and take' than a one-way sale, although it has not resulted in any coordinated purchases of important materiel. Instead, several broken-off projects were continued by Switzerland[2]. Not even the Swiss participation in the development of the Swedish rb-70 anti-aircraft missile resulted in a Swiss purchases of the final missile (Hagelin 1977).

These results should not necessarily be defined as failures. The rb-70 project seems to have been based primarily on Swiss technological interests, which reflect the larger military-industrial community in Switzerland compared to Finland and Austria. These interests may explain why Switzerland has been more interested than the other neutrals in cooperation with Sweden. This Swedish technological input into Swiss military industry might also explain the Swedish involvement in the projects which were later continued by Switzerland alone. To further emphasize this technological factor, there are suggestions of growing military demands in Switzerland for broader industrial participation on a European basis (*Aviation Week and Space Technology*, September 26, 1988, p. 11).

These findings point to more intricate reasons for neutral military trade than just a military need to acquire weapons. It has been argued that the main reason for the lack of any breakthrough in neutral military trade is that military acquisition plans as well as military demands have not been harmonized and that military industries are

too much alike (Tubin 1978, p. 35). The first part of the statement can
be confirmed by this book. The second part is more controversial. It can
be questioned, first, whether neutral military industries are alike. In
fact, the neutrals are not equals with regard to most military
indicators. Second, the most important factors may not be readily
quantifiable or measurable at all. Just as historic and cultural
similarities may explain military trade, they may also explain the
lack of such trade.

---

[1]It is a rule, sometimes even a necessity, to give a customer instructions in the
handling and support of important equipment. Finnish flight training during
the 1970s and Austrian training during the 1960s and 1980s were part of Swedish
foreign military sales to these countries. The Vidsel military proving ground just
south of the Arctic Circle is a test range that by its size is unique in Western
Europe. Several countries have used the range for different types of tests that
have not been related to Swedish foreign military sales. The Swiss Air Force
seems to be the only foreign Air Force to use the range regularly.

   Neither foreign training nor the use of the Vidsel range is defined as war
materiel sales. They are therefore not included in values presented in the
Swedish statistics. Both are, however, military services to foreigners and should
be included in any definition of military supplies. The same is true for different
types of international cooperation.

   In order to increase political control and industrial secrecy in international
cooperation while reducing bureaucratic delay and paperwork, Sweden has
signed bilateral government agreements (MoU, Memorandum of
Understanding) with most Western nations. A MoU refers in general to the
exchange of secret military information. In the MoU between Sweden and
Austria, signed in 1974, the term *military information* means messages,
documents and any kind of other basic data and materiel, whether or not they
are communicated orally, in writing, in the form of pictures, sound or an object.
Military information thus fits the definition of military supplies used in this
book.

   From what is known, Swedish-Swiss cooperation stands out as special. This
could explain the relatively high and stable Swedish sales to Switzerland. The
Swedish-Swiss MoU, when signed in 1966, was one of the first Swedish bilateral
military MoUs. The Swedish Ministry for Foreign Affairs in 1970 emphasized
the good political and military relations between the two countries (*Schweiz*
1970). The will to share information was said to be good on both sides. No
further clarification was given, but it can be assumed that it referred to the
Swiss financial and technical participation in the development of the Bofors
anti-aircraft rb-70 missile. Switzerland is so far the only neutral country known
to have been a partner in the research and development of important Swedish
military materiel.

   The statement in 1970 could also refer to another type of Swiss-Swedish
military cooperation. At the middle of the 1970s, Swedish and Swiss military
institutions established a study group for evaluating weapon systems and

threat perceptions. Results from military tests in Switzerland are made available to relevant Swedish authorities, such as the tests in 1975-1976 of the U.S. 'Dragon' anti-tank missile. In 1977-1978 the Hägglund light tank ikv91 was on loan to Switzerland for mountain tests. Such exchange can directly benefit both parties by giving valuable information about either foreign materiel or one's own materiel in a foreign environment. The Aeronautical Research Institute in Sweden also cooperates with Eidgenössische Flugzeugwerke to test aircraft designs, for instance the suggested but never materialized light attack aircraft B3LA and the JAS39 'Gripen' design.

It is evident that we are here walking the line between military exports and imports – cooperation is a matter of give and take. These are modes of military trade that lead to new and international division of labor. Instead of involving only goods in one-way sales, these modes are two-way and involve different types of military supplies. It is not always easy to conclude who gains the most. This is made all the more difficult because this type of cooperation is generally secret and therefore difficult to trace. It is not reflected in available foreign military sales statistics.

[2]The time period studied might give a somewhat distorted picture of the importance of different suppliers and cooperation partners. Even during a longer period, however, Switzerland stands out. For instance, it has been said that of the many foreign firms that during the past fifty years with their know-how and their products have contributed to the development of the Swedish air defense, Contraves has a special place (Herlitz 1980). Contraves was established as a private company in 1936 and is today wholly owned by the Oerlikon-Bührle Holding AG. Swedish trade with the company was established during World War II, when Sweden bought air defense fire support equipment. Other early Swiss materiel bought by Sweden was the m/41 Hispano-Suiza 20 mm aircraft cannon used in Sweden for both aircraft and airfield defenses. An improved cannon (m/47) was manufactured in Sweden from around 1948. Hispano-Suiza cannons were also used in Sweden on imported British fighter aircraft after World War II. 30 mm Oerlikon cannons were also installed in the 'Viggen' aircraft.

There are also examples of earlier Swedish support of Swiss R&D. The 'Super Fledermaus' system was originally developed by Contraves according to Swedish specifications during the late 1950s. After the Swedish Army eventually rejected it, Contraves concluded the project. In the early 1960s, Contraves and Oerlikon designed a 2 x 35 mm air defense gun system for the Hägglund & Söner bv202 personnel and over-snow vehicle. The project was canceled in 1965, but a modified gun tower equips 'Gepards' in the Federal Republic of Germany. Some years later Contraves proposed a solution for new fire support equipment for Swedish air defense guns. The project came to nothing when the Swedish Army in the late 1960s decided to invest in anti-aircraft missiles rather than in new gun systems. Contraves again completed the project and the end product went into the 'Skyguard'.

5

Cooperation or Competition

Complete and watertight control requirements are difficult to construct. As long as the delicate political balance act between restricting and permitting foreign military sales exists, there will be loopholes, whether deliberate or unforeseen. One conclusion from the preceeding chapters is that neither a large number of control requirements nor a broad coverage guarantees a strict implementation. Demands by the brotherhood created by the armed neutrality policy, differences in the indigenous military industrial base, increasing costs of military production and changes in the international military market are important factors explaining neutral foreign military sales.

Could one way out of the dilemma be to restrict, or at least to direct, foreign military sales to the other neutrals as an alternative to global sales? That is the hope of those supporting a neutral alternative. Neutral military trade has, after all, a positive and legitimate 'ring to it'. Other neutrals are, or have at least until illegal sales clouded the political sky, been regarded by the neutral governments as uncontroversial recipients. The main reason is, of course, their common foreign and security policies.

This chapter will analyze the international dimension of global military competition among the neutrals in order to reach further insights into the possibilities for a neutral alternative. Because a neutral alternative should rely more upon neutral suppliers than upon other suppliers, the importance of foreign suppliers to neutral armament is analyzed first.

5.1   MAJOR FOREIGN SUPPLIERS

No official military *import* statistics exist in all of the neutrals. Instead, ACDA has here been used. Critique was expressed previously of ACDA data with regard to neutral foreign military *sales*. ACDA is, nevertheless, the only organization that publishes easily accessible time series of major suppliers to most countries of the world. Tables 5.1-5.3 show that the United States is a military supplier to all the neutral countries. Not only that – it has by far been *the* most important foreign military supplier to three of the four neutral countries. This is an important part of the explanation why the neutrals have not been able to withstand U.S. pressures for strategic controls.

Although the relative importance of the United States can also be supported by other statistics (see volumes of *World Armaments and Disarmament*), the size of the U.S. share as presented by ACDA may nevertheless be exaggerated. It was noted previously, for instance, that commercial deliveries of items which may be intended for civilian use are included for the United States.

Another problem is whether the figures published by ACDA are adjusted in accordance with the wishes of the respective foreign governments or corrected in accordance with some other political consideration. On the one hand, if the published figures are adjusted to suit U.S. policy objectives, it seems likely that supply figures for the Soviet Union and the WTO will be overestimated in order to emphasize their military influence. With regard to neutral recipients, this is important only with respect to Finland. The share of Soviet deliveries to Finland has, however, decreased from the 1960s share.

On the other hand, figures of U.S. military sales may also be overestimated in order to show that other countries are not doing enough to support their own military security. This argument would apply mainly to NATO allies. It would therefore not be as important with respect to the neutrals because they are not involved in the NATO cost-sharing controversy.

It is impossible to reach a definite conclusion with regard to the treatment of the ACDA figures. Even though there are questions as to the reliability of these figures, it may be assumed that the relative importance of the United States is correct and that the relative size of other major military suppliers to the neutrals is correct enough to permit gross comparisons.

It was noted previously that Finland has more military recipients in the WTO, including the Soviet Union, than do the other neutrals. Finland is also the sole recipient of Soviet military materiel, inclu-

TABLE 5.1
Major foreign suppliers, 1965-1974 (million current $)*

	Soviet Union		United States		France		Great Britain		FRG		Canada		Others		Total	
Recipient	Sum	%	Sum	%	Sum	%	Sum	%	Sum	%	Sum	%	Sum	%	Sum	%
Austria	0	0	23	30	8	10	2	2	1	1	0	0	42	55	76	14
Finland	120	87	1	<1	1	<1	0	0	0	0	0	0	16	12	138	24
Sweden	0	0	80	61	0	0	18	14	14	11	0	0	18	14	130	22
Switzerland	0	0	138	57	10	4	61	26	14	5	0	0	16	6	239	40
Total	120	20	242	42	19	3	81	14	29	4	0	0	92	15	583	100

TABLE 5.2
Major foreign suppliers, 1975-1979 (million current $)*

	Soviet Union		United States		France		Great Britain		FRG		Canada		Others		Total	
Recipient	Sum	%	Sum	%	Sum	%	Sum	%	Sum	%	Sum	%	Sum	%	Sum	%
Austria	0	0	40	20	5	2	0	0	0	0	20	10	140	68	205	18
Finland	50	45	10	9	0	0	0	0	0	0	0	0	50	45	110	10
Sweden	0	0	140	58	5	2	10	4	0	0	0	0	90	38	245	22
Switzerland	0	0	460	80	0	0	10	1	0	0	10	1	100	18	580	50
Total	50	4	650	58	10	<1	20	1	0	0	30	2	380	34	1140	100

TABLE 5.3
Major foreign suppliers, 1981-1985 (million current $)*

	Soviet Union		United States		France		Great Britain		FRG		Italy		Others		Total	
Recipient	Sum	%	Sum	%	Sum	%	Sum	%	Sum	%	Sum	%	Sum	%	Sum	%
Austria	0	0	90	39	0	0	40	17	0	0	30	13	70	31	230	12
Finland	100	24	30	7	0	0	250	59	0	0	5	1	40	9	425	21
Sweden	0	0	300	67	5	1	100	22	0	0	5	1	40	9	450	23
Switzerland	0	0	700	80	20	2	0	0	0	0	0	0	160	18	880	44
Total	100	5	1120	56	25	1	390	20	0	0	40	2	330	17	1985	100

* Based on figures from the Arms Control and Disarmament Agency,
Department of State, Washington, D.C.

ding anti-aircraft missiles and fighter aircraft. The share of imports from the Soviet Union has declined, however, and during the 1981-1985 period was less than 50 per cent. It should also be noted that Finland seems to have lived up to the restriction not to buy war materiel from 'Germany'.

From the 1970s to the middle of the 1980s, the materiel acquisition share of Finland's military expenditures increased (Stenquist 1982). Although this increase partly reflected a deliberate ambition to strengthen the Finnish domestic defense industrial capacity, especially in the aircraft sector, it was also the result of purchases of British Hawk trainer aircraft. These purchases reduced, for the first time, the rank of the Soviet Union from the first to the second largest military supplier to Finland during the early 1980s. It is not unlikely that the Soviet share of Finland's military acquisitions will be further reduced. Recently Finland ordered a number of British Marconi 'Marksman' anti-aircraft systems (*Armed Forces Journal International*, February 1989, p. 44) and French 'Mistral' anti-aircraft missiles (*Defence & Armaments Heracles International*, November 1989, p. 8). During the 1990s new arcraft acquisitions are also planned. Two of the main contenders are new MiG fighters and the Swedish JAS39 'Gripen'.

The U.S. share increased during the 1980s to almost 70 per cent of total Swedish military imports. The Federal Republic of Germany has disappeared from the group of major suppliers, while the importance of Great Britain has increased. This illustrates that although Sweden is the major military producer among the neutrals, it has military demands that necessitate imports. Among imported supplies are sub-systems and components (mainly electronics), as well as some important materiel and technology.

Nevertheless, Switzerland is the major importer of U.S. materiel. Since the middle of the 1970s, the share has been as high as 80 per cent, which is the highest among the neutrals. Apart from air-to-air and anti-tank missiles, fighter aircraft explain the high U.S. share. F5E 'Tigers' make up the backbone of the Swiss fighter force. The U.S. F/A-18 'Hornet' was selected in 1988 as the follow-up to old British Hunters and Venom aircraft (*Aviation Week and Space Technology*, October 10, 1988, p. 30). The Swedish JAS39 'Gripen' was not an alternative due to its delayed delivery schedule. The U.S. share in Swiss imports has increased, and there is really no single second largest supplier. It is worth mentioning, however, that the delivery and manufacture of the Leopard tank have made the Federal Republic of Germany an important supplier of military technology to Switzerland.

Austria has had a more diversified import pattern. The Federal Republic of Germany is not a major supplier, although it is noted during the early period. Between 1965 and 1974, France was a major supplier, followed by Canada during the late 1970s. During the 1980s, both Great Britain and Italy became important suppliers (note that Italy has taken the place of Canada in table 5.3).

The differences between Austrian import patterns and those of the other neutrals are most likely due to the treaty restrictions in Austrian acquisitions and Austria's special military doctrine. Its military force structure is not as technology intensive as that of the other three countries. It was noted previously, for instance, that Austria has not until recently acquire guided missiles, which account for a relatively large part of the important materiel acquisitions of the other neutrals. Much of the Austrian military demands can be fulfilled from suppliers other than the United States.

A high concentration to a few major suppliers, with the exception of the latter part of the 1970s, is a common pattern among all the neutrals. One particular difficulty with the ACDA data is, however, that the category 'others' contains a rather large share of total imports. It is not specified how many 'other' suppliers are included in this figure. For Austria, that figure accounted for more than 50 per cent between 1965 and 1979, which is another illustration of the diversity of Austrian imports. On the basis of the foregoing analysis it can be concluded that some of the neutrals are among the other suppliers.

5.2   IF YOU CAN'T JOIN THEM

This book has not supported the thesis that neutrality as a policy has been important in shaping the actual trends in neutral foreign military trade. In fact, one may assume that international commercial competition has been just as important, perhaps even more important, than national control requirements in holding back an (in some cases even stronger) increase in foreign military sales. It is therefore no surprise that Swedish and Swiss firms are competitors on the international market (Tubin 1978). From the preceding analysis it may be suggested that as long as there is no *common* neutral policy of military trade, there is little chance that military producers and suppliers will cooperate *rather than compete*. Instead, they will base their activities on domestic demands and acquisition plans or, if these are not sufficient, on real or anticipated foreign demands. This will lead to competition rather than cooperation.

To what extent have neutral suppliers been competitors? Six possible outcomes of international military competition are outlined in figure 5.1. Suppliers A-D represent neutral countries. Suppliers E, F . . n are non-neutral competitors. Country X can be any recipient, thus also a neutral country. It will generally become known, sooner or later, that a particular neutral country has received an order for military materiel from country X (outcomes 1-4 and 6).

The difficult question to answer is how a contract was won. In accordance with the REFORMIS approach, negotiations may become known at an early stage, in effect during negotiations, if there is public and/or media awareness and concern of foreign military sales issues in any of the countries involved. But such awareness has generally been sporadic and late in most of the neutrals and even more so in other recipient states.

If there is a long negotiation process, if the deal is of particular importance to one of the countries or industries involved and/or if some illegalities have become known or been alleged, deliberate or accidental leaks of information are likely. This may explain why there is generally more information available when major powers are involved in military trade than when the competitors are non-aligned or other small states.

FIGURE 5.1
Alternative outcomes of international competition

Competing Suppliers	Neutral Suppliers	
Neutrals	(1) A selling to country X after competition with B-D (B-D are losers)	(2) B-D selling to country X without competition from A (A not participating)
	(3) A selling to country X without competition from B-D (B-D not participating)	(4) B-D selling to country X after competition with A (A is a loser)
Others	(5) A-D are losers to suppliers E, F . . . n in country X	
	(6) A-D are supplying country X after competition or in parallel with E, F . . . n	

Even so, in most cases when information is available before a supply contract has been signed, information generally appears in the later part of the negotiating process. At that stage only two or three competitors are normally still 'in the race'. This means that in most of the six outcomes in figure 5.1, it is not possible to conclude that A-D have participated and lost unless they have reached the final stage of the process or unless there is more information available than is normally the case. Given that the competition process from the first offer to the signing of the final contract is generally considered classified commercial information by the parties involved, the most common situation is that the information is not available until some time *after* the deal is completed. Even then, the information is not always complete.

Out of necessity, therefore, an attempt to analyze the outcomes must at best be based on scattered evidence, involving mainly important materiel. By systematizing the information in accordance with figure 5.1 one can nevertheless draw some general conclusions about the existence of neutral cooperation and competition. Because Sweden is the major neutral military producer and supplier, Sweden has been defined as 'country A'.

5.3   SIX OUTCOMES

Outcome 1

A Swedish producer supplies military materiel to country X after competition with other neutral producers. The best examples of this outcome are deals involving Bofors anti-aircraft guns and deals in which one of the losing competitors is Oerlikon from Switzerland. Both are major suppliers on the international market. George Thayer has concluded that they 'display an aggressiveness that stems more from self-interest than from government policy' (Thayer 1970, p. 303). The Bofors-Oerlikon competition was referred to by a former Director of Bofors at a conference in 1981 (*Folk och Försvar*, February 3, 1981): 'Oerlikon in Switzerland is with its 35 mm gun an extremely tough competitor for our 40mm gun, and has (a) politically easier (time) market(ing) it'.

One such outcome to the benefit of Bofors was the Divisional Air Defense (DIVAD) deal. In 1981 Bofors, teamed with Ford Aerospace, won the U.S. Army contract in competition with a similar cooperative venture involving Oerlikon (Hagelin 1985). Athough the contract was terminated in 1985 because of technical problems with the radar system, it was still good advertisement for Bofors.

Austria has also been a competitor with Sweden in deals involving Army materiel. When Bofors sealed the export order in 1986 covering the delivery of 155 mm field howitzers to India with the option of follow-up license manufacture, one of the main competitors was Voest-Alpine from Austria (*Dagens Nyheter*, May 4, 1984).

Among other categories of important supplies (guided missiles, jet aircraft, heavy tanks, submarines and other Navy ships), Switzerland could become a future competitor to Sweden as a result of its manufacture of the German Leopard tank. Should Finland go for an aggressive foreign military sales policy, it may become a possible competitor in surface ships. No major deals have been found, however, for which Sweden and Finland competed for the same major foreign contract. This fits the finding that Finland has not yet entered the international military market as a serious and determined supplier.

Outcome 2

A neutral country supplies military materiel to country X without Swedish competition. This is the most likely outcome in categories of equipment not developed in Sweden, such as advanced (non-jet) trainer aircraft, particular anti-aircraft systems, less sophisticated or specially designed armored vehicles, and small caliber guns and rifles. Due to the strong emphasis on jet fighter development in Sweden, no specially designed military non-jet trainer has been developed for many years.

Examples of armored vehicles without Swedish competition are the Swiss Piranha, the Austrian Küirassier and the Finnish Susi. During 1988, Sweden even bought a number of Susi vehicles for use by Swedish U.N. forces in the Middle East. A few Swiss armored vehicles were also bought in 1980 and 1981.

Because Sweden has continued to upgrade its traditional anti-aircraft guns and opted for guided missiles, anti-aircraft systems like the Swiss 'Fledermaus' or 'Skyguard' are not produced. This means that Sweden cannot compete within these categories of systems.

Light arms such as pistols and rifles are manufactured in Sweden mainly on licenses that generally do not allow re-exports to other countries. This means that Sweden cannot compete with, for instance, the Austrian firm Steyr, which has sold assault rifles to such countries as Oman, Saudi Arabia and El Salvador (*Defense & Armaments Heracles International*, March 1988, p. 6).

The probability of this outcome increases with increasing indigenous development in the neutral countries. For instance, instead of buying new foreign trainer aircraft, the Finnish Air Force acquired the indigenous L-70 trainer as a follow-up to previously imported Swedish Saab 'Safirs'. The Valmet company hoped that its successor to the L-70 trainer, the L-80TP (turboprop) 'Redigo', would be successful on the international market. The main competitors, as seen by the company, were the French 'Epsilon' and the Italian SF.260M aircraft. The heavier Swiss Pilatus PC-7 and PC-9 were considered less cost-effective by Valmet (*Aviation Week and Space Technology*, February 25, 1985, p. 105).

As it turns out, the 'Redigo' has been called a 'nightmare' for Valmet (*Dagens Nyheter*, June 16, 1989). It has killed two test pilots and has been difficult to sell. Instead, the two primary aircraft contenders in the category of light trainers on the international market are the Swiss PC-series and the Brazilian EMB-312. The Swiss PC-7 trainer has since its initiation in 1978 captured a major share of the international turboprop trainer market (*Aviation Week and Space Technology*, July 22, 1985, pp. 53-55). The PC-9 follow-up aimed not only at the same customers as those already using the PC-7, mainly in the Third World. Customers include Angola, Burma (Myanmar), Mexico and Saudi Arabia, possibly also Iran and Iraq. The PC-9 also won the Australian Aircraft Consortium, Ltd., Wamira primary Air Force trainer competition (*Aviation Week and Space Technology*, August 5, 1985, p. 24), and has made an entry into the U.S. military market (*Aviation Week and Space Technology*, April 28, 1986, p. 13).

The direction of sales is a second factor keeping Sweden out of much of neutral competition. Even when there exists overlap in neutral military production, Finland, Switzerland and Austria officially sell to countries in regions so far excluded from legal Swedish sales. Several such customers have been mentioned. In addition, Syria has bought a large number of Austrian armored personnel carriers (*Strategy Week*, June 2, 1980, p. 9). Switzerland's second largest military customer in 1985 was Saudi Arabia, and the fifth was Bahrain. Among the Air Forces using the PC-7 are Iran and Iraq (*Aviation Week and Space Technology*, August 5, 1985, p. 24). Moreover, Pilatus is the sole manufacturer of the German designed MBB-223K 'Flamingo' trainer, reportedly sold to Iraq and Syria (*Strategy Week*, June 2, 1980, p. 8).

Oerlikon 20 mm cannons and Steyr vehicles have been supplied to Saudi Arabia in great quantities as part of the U.S. Army program to modernize the Saudi Arabian National Guard (SANG) since 1973. The SANG today has one of the largest armored car forces in the world tailored for combat. The Oerlikon gun, mounted on a Cadillac Gage V150 car, is bought by the United States and supplied to Saudi Arabia under the U.S. Foreign Military Sales program (Kelleher 1985). Similarly, the sales of PC-9 aircraft to Saudi Arabia are part of a British deal to supply mainly the 'Tornado' fighter aircraft to that country (*World Armaments and Disarmament* 1988).

Outcome 3

A Swedish firm is supplying military materiel to country X without neutral competition. This outcome is most clear-cut in cases involving deliveries of military supplies that are not produced in the other neutral countries. This is often the case with Swedish deliveries of important equipment to other industrialized countries, including other neutrals. As already mentioned, Austria has ordered the Swedish 'Bill' anti-tank missile. Sweden is also a main supplier of armament and other supplies to the new Finnish missile-armed Fast Attack Craft. Each craft will be equipped with one Bofors 57 mm anti-aircraft gun, Saab Missile's rbs-15 anti-ship missile system, and Philips 9LV200 Mk2 fire-support and C^3I system. The Bofors rbs-70 anti-aircraft missile system is also under consideration by the Finnish Navy.

Other cases involve non-neutrals. The 'Bill' has been ordered by the U.S. Army. Light anti-tank weapons produced by the FFV, such as the Carl Gustaf and the AT-4, have been sold to a large number of countries. The customers for the rbs-70 anti-aircraft missile system include Norway, Pakistan and Australia. In Australia it will – just as in Sweden – replace U.S. 'Redeye' shoulder-launched missiles. Australia may become one of Sweden's major markets. In 1987, Kockums, the Swedish submarine producer, won the competition for the next Australian submarine. The main competitor was from West Germany. The contract, defining the project as a cooperative deal, involved both sales of submarines and license manufacture, and the contract was split among Swedish, Australian and U.S. suppliers. In addition, Bofors Electronics in 1989 together with Ericsson won the so called Amecon-consortia, a contract to equip Australian surface ships with radars, countermeasures and fire support (*N-Syntesen* 1989, no. 4).

At the same time there were several instances in which Sweden lost a potential contract to major suppliers (Hagelin 1979). The submarine contract with Australia was the first Swedish submarine sale abroad. Sweden has not succeeded in selling the most sophisticated weapon systems abroad, such as the 'Viggen' aircraft or the S-103 main battle tank. The main explanations for this failure seems to be the high level of sophistication and price, reflecting particular Swedish design demands (the 'Swedish profile'). Moreover, potential industrialized customers are either producing similar supplies themselves or are strongly guided by policy in their acquisition policies (see discussion of outcome 5). Other possible recipients, such as rich countries in the Third World, are often unlegitimate recipients. An additional reason is that high technological demands, indigenous development and dependence upon the importation of selected important supplies sometimes cause delay. This was the official reason the Swedish JAS39 'Gripen' was not a contender in the competition for a new fighter in Switzerland.

Outcome 4

Swedish suppliers lose in competition with a neutral supplier in country X. This is the opposite to outcome 1. As mentioned previously, DIVAD deliveries to the U.S. Army were stopped in 1985 due to technical difficulties with the radar system. A Bofors-Canadian Marconi team then competed for a new low level air defense weapon system for both U.S. and Canadian forces with Oerlikon-Bührle (teamed with Litton of Canada and Martin Marietta) and Swiss Contraves (teamed with Raytheon Canada), which had its Skyguard system and Oerlikon guns. As long as Bofors did not win, therefore, Oerlikon would. And so it did. First delivery of the Oerlikon-Martin Marietta system was to begin in 1988 for deployment at two Canadian airfields and ground force bases in the Federal Republic of Germany (*Aviation Week and Space Technology*, July 7, 1986, p. 13). In 1988 the Swiss-U.S. system also won the U.S. competition (*World Armaments and Disarmament* 1988, p. 188).

An interesting twist to the Canadian deal was implied by a highly placed Bofors employee in 1986. During an interview with the author, he stated that the Swedish loss was of no importance to Bofors because Bofors had recently won the India howitzer deal. He said, 'It was Switzerland's turn – we usually get every other contract' (we will return to this remark in outcome 6).

Outcome 5

Neutral suppliers are unsuccessful in country X against the competition from non-neutral producers. This has been a most common result in deals in which the major Western suppliers have participated with their most sophisticated materiel. Since the 1970s, additional competition has come from Third World countries such as Brazil, India, Israel and South Africa, which have managed to apply military technologies better suited for customers in the Third World.

NATO members buy most major weapons from each other or, more correctly, from the United States. It is often debated within NATO that there is, as among the neutrals, a one-way trade from the largest producer(s) to the smaller members. The major suppliers (the United States, Great Britain, France, the Federal Republic of Germany and Italy) often have the advantage of large stocks, political support that permits foreign military sales to be used as a foreign policy tool and the ability to give more favorable financial offers than is possible for the neutral governments.

Sweden has experienced these effects. In 1974-1975 Saab, as well as French and British competitors, lost against the United States in 'the arms deal of the century' (Dörfer 1983). Other attempts to sell the Viggen have all failed. Saab lost against British and French competitors for the supply of jet trainers to Finland and Belgium in the late 1970s (Hagelin 1979). Sweden lost to West Germany in an attempt to supply submarines to India in the late 1970s. The cases are many in which Swedish producers, as well as other neutral firms, have had to accept that others have managed to secure a major deal.

There are not many known deals in which several neutral producers have competed in the same deal and lost to a non-neutral competitor. This might be explained by a lack of public interest and therefore of public information – if they lost, why bother to write about it? Another explanation is that product specialization in the neutral countries limits the areas of overlap, both with regard to weapon categories and recipients. It was noted previously that few non-neutral countries are major recipients of military supplies from two or more neutrals. Neutral competition will undoubtedly increase if the neutrals decide to support continued military production by increasing foreign military sales, if international military competition continues, if the neutrals broaden their indigenous production and if they do not agree to cooperate rather than to compete.

Outcome 6

Several neutrals supply military materiel to country X with or without competition from other countries. This outcome can be of at least four types:

• the recipients may be the same for all the neutrals but at different times;
• neutral suppliers deliver materiel to country X separately but at the same time;
• the neutrals coordinate their deliveries; or
• they sell equipment that has been jointly produced.

In general, there is normally only one supplier of a specific type of important materiel to a particular country at a certain time. It has already been concluded that only a few major recipients are identical among the neutrals. Over time, however, as well as with regard to smaller recipients, the situation is different. From Appendix D it is evident that several recipients have bought military supplies from more than one neutral supplier. A non-neutral recipient can therefore, over time, buy from more than one of the neutrals.

At particular times, however, different branches of the armed forces in a recipient country might demand similar equipment. Neutral suppliers may in such cases supply different types of equipment to the same recipient country. Bofors 40 mm or 57 mm guns and Oerlikon 35 mm guns can be used, for instance, by the same country for different purposes. They can, for instance, be used by the Navy and the Army in different configurations. As was noted this is, for instance, the case in Finland. Similarly, while the Brazilian Air Force uses Swiss armaments on its 'Xavante' armed trainer aircraft, the Navy uses Bofors guns on license-manufactured British destroyers (*World Armaments and Disarmament* 1977, pp. 196-197).

Deliveries under such conditions do not demand any deliberate coordination of deliveries from the neutrals. The deal is organized by the buyer. More coordinated deals are contracts involving different neutral suppliers as both main and sub-contractors in the same deal with country X. For instance, Bofors and Contraves are both involved in India to incorporate Swiss fire-control radars on Bofors L/70 anti-aircraft guns (Hagelin 1985). Similarly, Ericsson supplies doppler modification kits to the Contraves' 'Fledermaus' fire support system which has been sold to more than two thousand customers (Herlitz 1980).

   The modification of materiel is today becoming increasingly common. Many modern military systems are constructed as 'building blocks' which permit modernization through the exchange of individual components or sub-systems (Hagelin 1985; *Defense & Armaments Heracles International*, June 1989). This 'cannibalization' is especially common with regard to electronic sub-systems. Another explanation is that arms deals are more and more becoming 'package deals' involving not only goods but also technology and know-how. As a result of the building block principle, different suppliers, even from different countries, can be involved in the negotiation stage with country X.
   The fourth type of outcome has, as far as is known, never occurred. The reason is that no important materiel sold abroad is known to have been developed through the cooperation of industries in two or more neutrals.
   To sum up: Despite the drawbacks already mentioned with regard to lack of information, examples involving the neutrals have been found in all of the six outcomes. In general, the neutrals are competitors rather than partners on the international market. But the forms of competition, as well as the categories of materiel involved, differ:

• The presentation supports the conclusion that Finland has not yet established itself as an important military supplier on the international market;
• Sweden does not yet experience strong neutral competition in most categories of important materiel. Instead, the main competitors are major Western producers. The exceptions are mainly air defense guns (Switzerland) and heavy Army artillery (Austria);
• when comparing categories of weapons produced in the neutrals, however, competition 'ought to' include personnel carriers and light armored vehicles (all the neutrals), heavy tanks (Sweden and Switzerland), light tanks (Sweden and Austria), non-jet trainer aircraft (Finland and Switzerland) and ships (Sweden and Finland). With regard to Swiss sales of heavy tanks, it remains to be seen whether the Swiss manufactured Leopard 2 tank can enter the international market in competition with sales directly from the Federal Republic of Germany. The international market for light armored vehicles seems diversified enough for the neutrals not to get involved in fierce competition;
• Sweden cannot compete with the other neutrals in certain categories of materiel such as advanced non-jet trainer aircraft, certain air defense systems, small caliber weapons and handguns manufactured

on licenses not permitting re-transfers, or in sales to certain regions of the world.

It is not always easy to establish the line between competition and cooperation. It is possible to 'cooperate by complementarity' as illustrated by outcome 6, in which a foreign *national* market is shared by way of product differentiation. For the neutrals to share *regional* foreign military markets in any formal way, however, seems impossible for several reasons. First, such an alternative probably implies that neutral foreign military sales have become an important foreign policy tool. Second, the neutrals do not account for large market shares in most important categories of materiel or regions; they do not 'control' any larger foreign markets. Attempts by the neutrals to share regional foreign markets would therefore have to take into account competition from non-neutrals.

Third, because the neutrals do not generally cooperate, such an agreement seems impossible. The view by the Bofors employee quoted in outcome 4, however, points to a possible exception to these conclusions. In the beginning of this section it was suggested that as long as there is no common neutral political agreement explicitly supporting neutral military trade, competition will be the most likely result. Generally, the international military market since the 1970s has been characterized as 'a buyer's market' due to the growing number of suppliers offering an increasing variety of military supplies as well as modes of trade. Competition as well as distrust normally prevents agreements among suppliers (see Schandler et al. 1977).

The powder cartel discovered during the 1980s can therefore be considered a relatively rare phenomenon. Or can it? Sometimes competition is basically limited to two suppliers of a similar type of major equipment. Such is the case with anti-aircraft guns. Bofors and Oerlikon are the two major holders of the world's anti-aircraft gun market in the calibers 35-57 mm. Such a market situation has been extensively studied in economic theory as a sort of monopoly. But this situation has also interested cooperation and conflict 'game' theorists. One question that has been studied is in what situations two parties might cooperate rather than compete. Different games, such as the 'prisoner's dilemma' and 'mixed-motive' games, have been constructed in order to answer this question (Rapoport 1960; Axelrod 1980; Boulding 1982; Schellenberg 1982). To summarize the findings of these sometimes very intricate theories, it seems that in certain situations and under certain conditions both parties will gain by cooperation, especially in the long run.

Although it is impossible without access to 'inside' documents to verify that such 'cooperation by competition' exists between Bofors and Oerlikon, a 'tit-for-tat' agreement (Axelrod 1980) – if I make this deal, you make the next – fits the statement by the Bofors employee referred to previously. This explanation implies that there is, in fact, more neutral military cooperation than can be deduced from the quantitative data or than may even be known by the respective governments.

Such covert, perhaps even illegal, cooperation is not, however, the type of cooperation that should be sought in a neutral alternative. In the final chapter we shall discuss how such an alternative might be attained.

6

Conclusions and Discussion

6.1 SUMMARY

Neutral foreign policy creates expectations of a restrictive foreign military sales policy. At the same time, economic and technological demands make it difficult to sustain an advanced, indigenous, armed neutrality policy without continued or even increasing foreign military sales. These factors have put the neutral governments in a dilemma: how to support indigenous military production by way of foreign military sales while fulfilling expectations of restrictive foreign military sales.

The REFORMIS approach was developed to investigate this dilemma and compare neutral foreign military sales policies. The approach distinguishes between formal military sales policy and actual foreign military sales. A military-industrial-political brotherhood in all the neutrals pushes for continued indigenous military production and, if need be, foreign military sales.

A restrictive formal policy was considered the result of public demands for additional and more comprehensive control requirements and the government's recognition of the legitimacy of such demands. The operationalization of formal policy in accordance with the REFORMIS approach comprises the foreign military sales control requirements; the more control requirements and the broader their coverage, the more restrictive is the formal policy. Actual foreign military sales reflect the implementation of formal policy. This is operationalized through the value of military sales and the number and relative shares of recipients and regions.

From an empirical comparison of national control requirements we conclude that Sweden is the neutral country with the most restrictive formal policy. The other three countries reflect less restrictive formal policies. For actual foreign military sales to be in accordance with formal policy, a strict implementation of formal policy is necessary. By combining the options of a more or a less restrictive formal policy with the options of a strict or loose implementation of the control requirements, four possible foreign military sales outcomes are defined. The two outcomes representing strict implementation of formal policy are those which should be expected of the neutrals: a Restraint outcome (A) for Sweden and a Domestic Policy Tool outcome (C) for the other neutrals. With a loose implementation of either a more or a less restrictive formal policy, the outcomes are B (Legitimization) and D (Business as Usual), respectively.

The characteristics of the Restraint outcome are:

- No domestic production mainly for foreign customers;
- a constantly low and/or reduced value of global military sales as well as number of recipients over time;
- no military sales to countries in zones of conflict or to parties engaged in international conflict or war;
- non-existent or low values of foreign military sales to members of military alliances in Europe or, alternatively, balanced foreign military sales to members of NATO and the WTO in order not to discredit a non-aligned foreign policy;
- relatively more sales to neutral recipients than to non-neutrals.

The Domestic Policy Tool outcome represents a less restrictive but nevertheless strictly implemented formal policy. Due to less coverage of the control requirements, the value of foreign military sales and the number of recipients are expected to be higher than in the Restraint outcome. The indicators should not, however, reflect constant increases over time.

Two initial findings point out the risk of drawing far-reaching conclusions about a nation's foreign military sales policy on the basis of only a single indicator: Sweden's restrictive formal policy and the low and stable value of Finland's foreign military sales. On the basis of the total number of indicators, both countries reflect a loose implementation of formal policy.

The major sign of restraint found in Sweden's actual military sales is that direct military sales to countries in main zones of conflict such as southern Africa and the Middle East do not occur. With regard to the other indicators, Sweden is the clearest example of a contradiction between formal policy and actual military sales. The formally more restrictive foreign military sales policy in Sweden has not prevented an increase in most foreign military sales indicators. It has even been acknowledged by the Swedish government that policy implementations have been loose. Moreover, the minor court sentences for the individuals involved in illegal sales have shown that the export law itself is ambiguous and difficult to implement. In connection with the presentation of the new control requirements in 1988, it was stated that the new guidelines should be implemented more strictly in the future (*Press Release* 1988a, p. 2). In other words, they had not been implemented strictly until then.

The same general conclusions are true for Switzerland and Finland (figure 6.1). Switzerland shows a relatively constant, although high, value of total foreign military sales. The bias toward NATO reci-

FIGURE 6.1
The neutrals according to the REFORMIS outcomes*

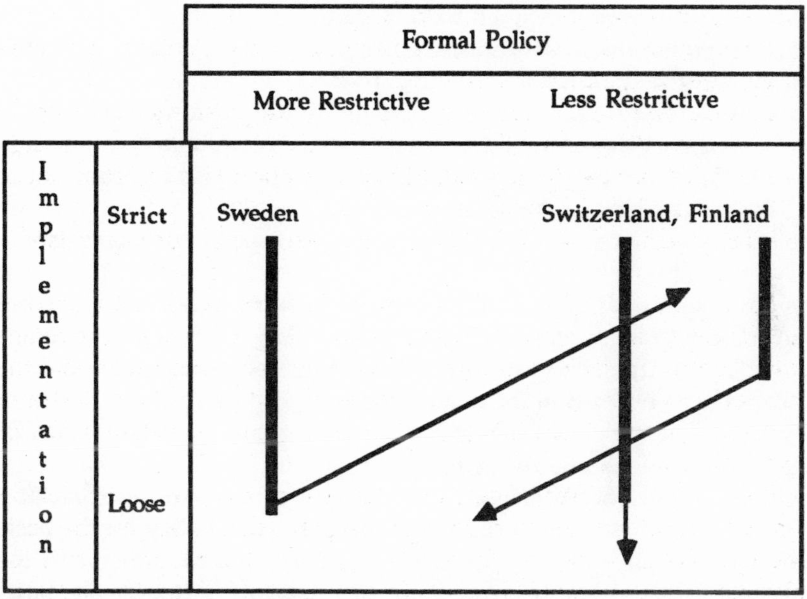

* The broader arrow indicates the direction in which the neutrals have moved away from the expected outcomes according to the REFORMIS analysis. The narrow arrow indicates a possible future direction of policy.

pients is especially pronounced in war materiel sales from Switzerland. For both Switzerland and Finland there are indications that they have taken advantage of zones of conflict in order to increase their foreign military sales. The increase found in the number of recipients from Switzerland, especially in the Middle East, can be explained by the change in implementation of foreign military sales policy in 1978.

The empirical investigations showed that the neutrals reflect a strict implementation of formal policy only to a limited extent (in accordance with outcomes A and C). Although some individual producers are involved in projects mainly for foreign customers, only Austria has on a national level had military production mainly for foreign customers (in accordance with outcome D). It is not possible, therefore, to clearly define the neutral countries in one outcome or the other. That is why the direction away from the expected outcome rather than a definite position has been illustrated in figure 6.1.

Sweden and Switzerland clearly illustrate a gap between formal policy and actual foreign military sales. The solutions to the dilemma have been different, however. In Sweden the government seems not to have taken the dilemma seriously. The acceptance of public demands for more restrictions has not been regarded as contradictory to demands for more military sales. In its attempts to support domestic production, the Swedish government has opted for a hidden and pragmatic solution and has implemented the control requirements loosely.

In Switzerland a loose implementation of formal policy was politically accepted in 1978. This reflects an open acceptance of the dilemma. The fact that the control requirements in Switzerland have much less coverage than in Sweden could indicate a Swiss 'laissez-faire' policy in foreign military sales. The 1978 decision is in accordance with such a conclusion. The Swiss solution has been clear and has been enacted in the open through a political decision.

According to the REFORMIS approach, the main explanation of the loose implementation of formal policy in all the neutrals is the political importance attached to indigenous military production and the anticipated benefits from foreign military sales. This explanation fits the Swedish case especially well. Sweden has the broadest military industrial base among all the neutrals. Sweden develops important military supplies that are not developed or even manufactured by the other neutrals. Sweden has, contrary to the other neutrals, historically been involved in an international military 'technology race'. At the same time, Sweden has the most restrictive formal foreign military sales policy.

Another important explanation relates to the functions of the control requirements in foreign military sales policy. The REFORMIS outcomes were developed around the ideal Restraint (outcome A). That outcome is based upon indicators of actual foreign military sales that are theoretically defined from the expectations of a strict implementation of formal policy. Formal policy, in turn, is based upon the number and coverage of the control requirements. They are assumed to be the result of governmental arbitration, i.e., a least common denominator between the demands for a more permissive and a more restrictive foreign military sales policy. Most importantly, the control requirements are mainly *conditional* requirements. This means that they are indications of a 'best general direction' for the implementation of policy.

It may be wrong, therefore, to expect that actual sales will in every instance fullfill formal control requirements as long as indigenous military production is politically supported. Thus, in order to solve the dilemma, an increase in the number of control requirements is not sufficient. Instead, a strict implementation of formal policy is necessary. To accept more and increasing coverage by the control requirements may therefore, without a strict implementation, increase the dilemma.

This conclusion is important when discussing the future. Neutrality in the four studied countries is not an identical policy. Although they do not necessarily contradict, they sometimes cross. This situation does not benefit the creation of a neutral alternative in military trade. In fact, a restrictive foreign military sales policy in support of the basic attitudes outlined in chapter 1 seems more and more difficult to implement. The paradoxical conclusion is that not even an increasing number of control requirements is a sufficient condition for reducing foreign military sales.

If we confine ourselves to the domestic situation, i.e., leaving the effects of international competition aside, more control requirements have been suggested in Finland partly in order to be able to control increasing foreign military sales. This might seem like a contradiction. According to the findings, however, it is not an impossible outcome. An increase in foreign military sales is supported by the Finnish Foreign Trade Association (*Defence Equipment from Finland* 1988). Without a concerned public opinion that is aware of the distinction between formal policy and its implementation, Finland may attempt to move toward the Legitimization outcome (B).

In Switzerland the situation is different. The political decision in 1978 to accept a loose implementation of formal policy meant that the position of the military-industrial-political brotherhood was strengthened. The critical public opinion automatically found itself in a more difficult position than before. A Parliamentary Commission in 1988 decided to investigate Swiss foreign military sales policy. Although the report may suggest increases in the number of control requirements, any drastic increase in their total coverage seems unlikely. The value of Swiss foreign military sales in 1988 was reduced compared to the 1987 figure (see Appendix C), which may increase demands for even less government involvement in foreign military sales. It seems likely that the Swiss government will try to consolidate outcome D.

The future in Austria is difficult to predict because there is so little statistical information to go on. Austria has therefore not been included in figure 6.1. One alternative for the Austrian government would be to consolidate its military production as a means to support domestic demands (outcome C). Another would be to follow the Swiss example: to officially accept a loose implementation of foreign military sales control requirements and sell to almost any foreign customer when the chance appears. It seems likely, however, that the foreign market for Austrian military supplies will remain limited; therefore the latter option may be difficult to realize.

The Swedish position does not seem stable. During 1988, the value of total foreign military sales continued to increase. Changes are likely to occur. But in which direction? Outcome A is most strongly demanded by the peace movements. But the increased coverage by recent control requirements has left them very much in limbo and without momentum. Investigations are presently studying the role of foreign military sales and international cooperation in Swedish military production, on the one hand, and the definition of war materiel, on the other. Until these investigations present their results, there seems to be no defined foreign military sales issue to fight *against*. This has left the military-industrial-political brotherhood with the upper hand in its demands for a less restrictive policy.

Recent information indicates that slightly more than 50 per cent of total Swedish production of war materiel was supplied to foreign customers in 1988. This reflects a movement toward outcome D. But that outcome is much too drastic as a long-term solution. It does not take into account the need for strict implementation which has been acknowledged by the government. Foreign military sales as a Domestic Policy Tool (outcome C), however, combine strict implementation with a less restrictive formal policy. The number of members of the Swedish Parliament with roots in the peace activities of the 1950s and 1960s has been reduced. New members do not necessarily have as strong a peace commitment. Many are tired of the issue of foreign military sales after the many 'affairs' of the 1980s. Instead, European and environmental issues seem more important in the politics of today as well as for the immediate future.

This situation may very well reduce the opportunities for the critical opinion to find media and Parliamentary support for more restrictive foreign military sales policies. In Sweden an unofficial suggestion has already been presented which introduced two main control criteria and put more emphasis upon the government and its 'total assessment' (*Medborgarkommissionens rapport* 1988, pp. 243-244). In effect, these developments indicate that the brotherhood has continued political support. The linkage between sustained indigenous military production and foreign military trade will probably be more strongly and more openly acknowledged by the Swedish government in the future.

If there is predictive power in the REFORMIS approach, we may in the future see Finland trying to move toward outcome B, Sweden toward outcome C and Austria toward outcome C or possibly D, with Switzerland trying to consolidate its present policy (outcome D). Whether this will be successful or not depends not only upon domestic push and pull but also upon the neutrals' international competitiveness. Developments in foreign military markets and (re)actions by neutral as well as other producers become important. Are the neutrals willing to accept, for instance, new modes of trade and perhaps also offer tailor-made products for foreign customers? Will military production and sales continue to be made from mainly home-based companies, or will production and sales originate from facilities abroad? In general, it may be assumed that international market forces will play a more decisive role in the future, thereby sharpening the neutral dilemma.

There is clearly a risk that the legitimacy of a neutral foreign policy in general, as well as of neutral military sales in particular, may be further undermined without a radical change in foreign military sales policies and implementation. The neutral dilemma grows with the gap between negative effects from foreign military sales and the expected role of neutral foreign and security policies. Foreign military sales result in increased global armament and perhaps also in increasing political and military temptations by the recipients to use their military arsenals. In parallel with new modes of trade, the possibilities for international control of global armament are reduced (Hagelin 1984). This situation complicates and even contradicts the neutral foreign policy goals of peaceful conflict resolution and international arms control and disarmament.

There has not been a politically supported and deliberate concentration of foreign military sales to the other neutrals. With few exceptions, bilateral neutral trade has been unimportant. The neutrals are competing internationally as much as they are trading with each other. Major powers are generally more important as military suppliers to particular neutrals than are the other neutrals. Likewise, Western industrialized countries are as important, sometimes more important, recipients of military supplies from the neutrals than are the neutrals themselves.

The main explanations to the described situation seem to be that:

* Military trade has mainly been a commercial activity managed by industry instead of being an actively implemented governmental policy;
* military production in the neutral countries is specialized but not to an extent that has abolished neutral competition or competition with non-neutral suppliers;
* in no neutral country is there any visible political will to control what has here been defined as military supplies as opposed to war materiel. Sales of military supplies are accepted without taking into account the negative long-term international consequences.

This explains why there are contradictory political perspectives with regard to military imports and military sales. Whereas military imports are generally free and uncontrolled (in Sweden only imports from South Africa are controlled), military sales involve control requirements. At the same time, the importation of military supplies has traditionally been regarded as the most important threat to national independence and neutral credibility.

This is an interesting paradox in military trade relations and their assumed security importance that has generally not been recognized. The neutral dilemma created by indigenous military production has increased the demands for military imports, foreign military sales and new modes of international production and trade. None of these can be treated as separate issues; they are facets of the same general difficulty of how to afford national armament. Foreign military sales are treated as necessary in order to sustain indigenous production. At the same time, national armament cannot, for economic and technological reasons, take place without the purchases of military supplies from abroad.

Being dependent upon – i.e. in this case having important military import as well as export relations with – another government may mean a loss of freedom of action. Already Machiavelli, writing *The*

Prince in 1512, perceived the principle that power grows out of the dependence of others. This has since become a leading idea in 'realist' international political theories. One view in the military dependence debate is that the biggest risks for international military dependence occur when a small country has military relations with a major power (Hagelin 1986). Subsequently, if relations between non-major powers grow, relations with major powers can change both relatively and quantitatively in a direction that will benefit small powers (Wallensteen 1973, p. 90). The risks are reduced if a small nation has military relations with several countries. Preferably they should not be major powers. One example is the Swedish argument that Third World countries in particular are better off buying weapons from Sweden than from, say, the United States, because they will then avoid the 'political strings' attached to major-power military sales. The same conclusion ought, then, to be true for every other country, including the neutrals.

From this it follows that freedom of action is not much reduced unless the relations are multiplied with states other than the United States, the Soviet Union, Great Britain, the Federal Republic of Germany, Italy or France. It was shown previously that these powers are among the main foreign suppliers to the neutrals. Moreover, at least one major power is among the major neutral recipients. The conclusion is that all major foreign military trade relations of the neutrals would have to change.

6.2   NEUTRAL ALTERNATIVES

It is clear that no future alternative involving closer relations among the neutrals, whether in military or other spheres, will come about easily. The neutrals have to clarify and specify their international role. A neutral alternative in military trade requires not only that the national foreign military sales control requirements be extended and made more identical, but that they be actively implemented. Active government involvement, guidance, steering and support seem of paramount importance for changing military trade policies. To illuminate the complexity, it is worth repeating that:

- It is not sufficient to increase the number of foreign military suppliers as long as the military demands in the neutral countries are such that the major powers remain the only possible suppliers of important supplies;

- if major suppliers are allied to one of the superpowers from which they attempt to increase military independence, the solution(s) cannot be considered successful;
- Western European countries have accepted military-industrial cooperation as a way out of both military dependence upon the United States and national economic and technological constraints. The neutrals have so far *excluded* participation in NATO or WTO multinational military projects as a politically acceptable policy;
- neutral military demands have thus to change in a direction that will permit other than major powers to fill the military demands and that will not exclude international cooperation. From a political point of view the neutrals are the most logical choice.

Today, the rate of new independent nations per year has been sharply reduced compared to the decolonization period of the 1960s. Military demands by Third World countries slowed down during the 1980s (*World Armaments and Disarmament* 1986, 1987). Global military sales may be moving toward a more 'normal', i.e., reduced, level than during the 1960s and 1970s. Gaining new recipients, therefore, generally means taking market shares from competitors. This will be difficult unless the supplier is prepared to lower the price, offer supplies that are better suited for the recipient's demands than those offered by competitors, offer economic or other benefits in excess of one's competitors or turn to previously unacceptable customers.

For the neutrals, these alternatives cannot be realized unless the supplier government is involved politically as well as financially to a larger extent than at present. Successful competition will in the future most likely continue to depend upon an appropriate product design, competitive price and timing. A producer which can offer less advanced and/or cheaper military products may in fact be better off than one which can offer only the most advanced supplies. The so called Swedish profile, i.e., materiel specialized for particular Swedish military demands, is not necessarily a competitive advantage on markets in which materiel has to be cheap and rugged rather than slick and expensive.

A neutral alternative can be defined in the short as well as in the long term. It can be described as a military or as a non-military alternative. There is therefore no such thing as *a* neutral alternative. Four alternatives, each a successive transformation from the present situation, are discussed in the following sections. In three of the four alternatives the neutral role is still mainly military. The last alternative describes a transformation away from the present armed neutrality toward a new neutral role.

Go It Alone

This is the most 'nationalistic' of the four alternatives. The military and political frame of reference in each of the neutrals is based upon traditional national foreign and security policies. National security is to be achieved by individual armament policies. Indigenous military R&D is considered the best policy, but foreign supplies are bought whenever necessary. In this alternative, neutral military trade is low, and it is not actively directed. The political aim is to support indigenous production by as little interference in commercial activities as possible.

This alternative is, by and large, what the preceeding pages have described. Where can the neutrals go from here? Two propositions can be formulated for a neutral armament alternative:

- The neutrals can probably benefit from closer military trade by sharing the costs of armament, especially in the development of important materiel, but
- the greater the changes necessary in relation to the present, the harder it will be to find a common solution.

The first proposition is based on economic theory. The examples so far of multinational R&D projects of important materiel show that it is more difficult to realize cost reductions in practice than in theory. Although shared by the partners, the national expenditures may be substantial and may even be too high. The second proposition is a practical one and means that increasing neutral military trade is easiest to achieve if the following conditions already exist:

- Military trade with non-neutrals does not contain important supplies;
- the share of neutral military trade in total military trade is high;
- military trade among neutrals is symmetrical ('fair'); and
- the content of neutral military trade is complementary and involves important materiel.

It has been shown that this is not the situation today. The issue of symmetry is of particular importance. It is a continually complicating issue in Atlantic military trade and can also be assumed to be an important ingredient in a successful and stable neutral alternative. There are at least two sides to the issue of neutral symmetry. First, neutral trade must be considered fair with regard to both benefits and drawbacks over time by all nations involved. Such benefits and drawbacks are measured not only in economic and industrial but also in technological, political and military terms. Second, there must be relatively more benefits in neutral military trade than can be gained by military trade with other countries. Only then can a neutral alternative withstand pressures and offers from non-neutral suppliers and recipients.

One conclusion is therefore that in order to make neutral military trade an *alternative to* the present situation, major changes have to occur. Only by a well-defined and well-formulated neutral policy (the Role), actively supported by the governments in each neutral country, can such an alternative be achieved. It is no easy solution. But step-by-step changes can set the direction. A first step could be to include coordinated military production and acquisition plans in the new discussions of strengthening neutral cooperation (*Dagens Nyheter*, October 29, 1989).

Coordination

Traditional security frames of reference and military-industrial-political brotherhoods are difficult to dissolve. National security in the Coordination alternative is still mainly achieved by armament based upon national policy. The national frames of reference are nevertheless harmonized by political guidelines in order to direct military acquisition more toward what the other neutrals can offer as well as need. Limited common military planning, perhaps on the lines of Swedish-Swiss cooperation, could be a step in this direction.

Coordination means limited policy guidance toward neutral military trade. The changes from the Go It Alone alternative are not great. The most important additional factor is stronger political involvement in guidance and support toward increasing inter-neutral sales and license manufacture. A first sign of political coordination could be for each neutral government to sign military trade MoUs with all the other neutral governments. It would strengthen the role of the MoU as a political instrument if the neutrals, instead of signing several bilateral MoUs, signed one multilateral MoU. It could be formulated as an 'intent' or even a promise to give special trading and offset treatment to neutrals. Political interference with commercial practices could be limited to categories of supplies in which neutral complementarity already exists. No binding coordination of national acquisition plans would be necessary, but neutral supplies should be considered first choice whenever the neutrals plan new important military acquisitions.

National acquisition plans should be harmonized. An example of what should not be allowed to happen in this alternative is illustrated by the recent fighter aircraft decision in Switzerland when the JAS39 'Gripen' was not considered due to the delayed production schedule. An example for the future is the acquisition of a new Swedish main battle tank. One of the foreign alternatives is the Leopard tank. It should be investigated whether Sweden could acquire the Leopard not from the Federal Republic of Germany but from Switzerland. The same situation exists with regard to present Swedish plans to acquire certain air defense missiles not produced in Sweden.

Yet another example involves a planned Swedish acquisition of new surface ships. Swedish producers have supplied much of the electronic equipment and armament to the new Finnish Fast Patrol Boats. These ships may fulfill the demands specified by the Swedish Navy. Finland is, at the same time, planning to acquire new fighter aircraft during the 1990s. One of the possible alternatives is the Swedish JAS39 'Gripen'. Thus, there exists a situation in which Swedish aircraft could be traded for Finnish ships, thereby relieving some of the strain upon Sweden's aircraft production and Finland's shipyards.

All of the neutrals could support a reduction in the remaining treaty restrictions on Finnish and Austrian armament. Although this is not a necessary condition for the Coordination alternative, it could ease armament coordination as well as 'pave the way' for the Integration alternative.

Another step could be for all the neutrals to be more explicit about and to harmonize their definition, interpretation and implementation of policy in peacetime and perhaps their neutrality in wartime. This step does not necessarily imply that Sweden should accept international guarantees of its neutrality, although that could be one alternative. An initial step could nevertheless be for all the neutrals to start discussing a least common denominator with regard to the interpretation of neutrality according to international law. It was suggested in section 1.1 that without respect for international law, neutrality is very much a policy without meaning. This will be especially important in the other alternatives described here.

Among the most important steps would be for all the neutrals to agree upon identical or at least common control requirements, to actively implement their foreign military sales policies and to publish similar or identical annual statistical reports about their foreign military trade. These reports should cover sales, imports and co-operation in different forms.

The present situation in Austria with regard to public information is especially regretable, but Finland could also make its foreign military sales statistics more easily accessible. All of the neutrals could make their statistics more complete. They could also present annual 'Conventional Arms Trade Impact Statements' similar to the ones that have existed for many years in the United States. These statements should be public, passed by the respective Parliaments and include a detailed presentation of the rationale(s) for selling military supplies to non-neutral recipients. Each neutral government should explicitly declare, by referring specifically to each recipient, why that particular recipient is better off buying military supplies from the neutrals than from some other supplier. The political aim should be to distance neutral policy from one of the most hypocritical arguments in support of one's own global foreign military sales – 'if we do not sell, someone else will'. Instead, the policy should be that 'if someone else can sell, let him'.

The main asymmetry among the neutrals today is the larger Swedish military industrial base and Sweden's wide spectrum of military R&D compared to the other neutrals. Coordination would therefore in the short term benefit Sweden the most because Sweden is the major neutral producer of important materiel. The Coordination alternative would therefore be unfair. But this alternative would be positive in the sense that Sweden could supply military supplies which are today purchased from non-neutral suppliers. Nevertheless, it means that Sweden in the long run would have to restructure its military industrial base more than the other neutrals would in order to meet neutral demands and create a stable and fair neutral alternative. The Coordination alternative is but a first step.

This situation mirrors the military trade relationship between the United States and its allies in Europe. Are there any lessons to be learned from NATO experiences in this regard? Yes, there probably are. When the United States has accepted foreign military materiel, it has always been manufactured on license in the United States. The main benefits are that a second source for the materiel is gained while some domestic employment and industrial benefits are upheld. The parallel would be for Sweden to accept more license manufacture of supplies from the other neutrals. Sweden should also reduce, perhaps even give up, some of its indigenous R&D capacity for supplies that could be manufactured on license from another neutral country.

License manufacture of mainly U.S. major weapons, both bilateral and multilateral (consortia) manufacture, has been successful in Western Europe compared to multinational R&D projects if the calculus includes acquisition costs, the number of weapons produced and the number of nations participating (Hagelin 1977). No R&D capacity is needed to participate in license manufacture, which makes it open to more nations than R&D projects do. Thus, not only Sweden but the other neutrals as well could consider license manufacture an alternative to direct imports or indigenous developments. It would strengthen the Coordination alternative if such manufacture were organized multinationally rather than bilaterally among the neutrals.

The distribution of benefits and drawbacks to each participant in multinational projects can be arranged within one or several projects during the same time frame or through distribution of tasks over time and among different projects. The more common are the projects, the better is the chance of reaching a fair distribution of benefits and drawbacks. The broad Swedish military R&D base means that although there are areas in which the neutrals could agree on common R&D projects, the common core for development projects is presently not very wide with regard to important materiel. The structural inequalities make it difficult to create symmetry within R&D projects. R&D cooperation therefore seems a delicate matter and should be left to the Integration alternative. In the Coordination alternative, common neutral projects should be confined to license manufacture.

The Coordination alternative as presented here will only reduce, but not replace, trade with major non-neutral suppliers. One effect might even be that in order to pay for increasing purchases from Sweden, the other neutrals might need to increase their foreign military sales to non-neutral recipients. To counter such a development, Swedish acceptance of offsets and other trading arrangements would be crucial.

Neutral competition will still remain on a global scale. Neutral trade in this alternative is based upon the easiest and least demanding solution with only limited political direction. No far-reaching change in national military acquisition and production plans is suggested. The main means by which to direct neutral military trade are political guidelines, offsets and license manufacture. Nevertheless, by coordinating neutral foreign military trade, the neutral governments would have agreed upon the first necessary condition – the vision of a common neutral role in creating an alternative to both major-power domination of neutral armament and neutral involvement in global armament.

Integration

A necessary condition in order to make neutral military trade a stable and long-term alternative is common neutral political support of maximum neutral trade and cooperation *at the expense* of military trade with other countries. It is not sufficient to import or license manufacture neutral supplies now and then; this must be the normal procedure. A neutral alternative must include a willingness to change one's own military production and acquisition policy to such an extent that it fits the total, combined, neutral military industrial structure and neutral military demands. There must be national rationalization and specialization in order to make combined neutral production and acquisitions efficient, fair and stable.

At the same time, the military demands must fit the possible output from this new neutral military production structure. It will be necessary for the military and the polity to change military ambitions, force structures and materiel content. Common, long-term acquisition plans and the harmonization of hitherto different security frames of reference must be formulated. The industries must be strongly circumscribed in their overall military trade relations. This alternative can be achieved only 'from above', i.e., by strong and active political direction and support.

This alternative is in some respects similar to the neutral Nordic alternative discussed during the late 1940s. Instead of individual, national armament policies, a *common neutral* peacetime armament policy should be formulated. Non-alignment in peacetime and neutrality in wartime are still the 'guiding star'. One could say, however, that a separate neutral alliance – a 'United Neutrals' – has to be established but without the planning for wartime operational cooperation of traditional military alliances. Only the planning for and production, acquisition, and trade of military supplies in peacetime are involved. The still national defense forces are created by emphasizing not national but integrated neutral military research, development, manufacture and trade.

The military demands clearly have to change. Military leaderships have a tendency to demand the latest and most advanced military technology. 'Enough' does not exist in their normal vocabulary. A continuing armament policy creates serious – not to mention insoluble – economical allocation difficulties in competition with other, likewise increasing social demands. Politically, any neutral alternative implies strong political direction and support. Policy must 'control' and actively implement not only neutral military trade but also national military demands. How?

The answer is found in international law. International law becomes in this alternative not only the basis for neutrality but the basis for neutral adaptation and armament as well as the neutral role. The military-political aim is here not to compete with international military technological developments in general or with armament policies of particular countries. Politically, it must be realized that there is no single and uncontroversial answer to the question 'How much is enough?'. In fact, it may be argued that the solution to national security has less to do with the amount or size of armament. Instead, the neutrals should in common define 'how *little* is enough'. This should be done by agreeing upon the *minimum* obligations of a neutral state in wartime in accordance with neutral interpretation of international law.

This task is as important as it is difficult for the realization of an integrated neutral alternative. By defining minimum obligations, the neutrals will not have to relate their armament policy to every new technological development. Defined together, these obligations will be recognized as neutral policy, not as a unilateral interpretation of international law by a single neutral government.

The armament policy should effectuate these minimum obligations. Military demands are thus 'contained' in the neutral interpretation of these obligations. Such is the new military-political goal. It will give legitimization to changed, even reduced, national military production. Although it is not possible to make that analysis here, it seems reasonable to assume that such a restructuring could include the so called non-offensive or defensive force postures much studied during the 1980s.

The national military forces are mainly to be created from the common resources available in the neutral countries. The neutrals make up the major military market. In the most clear-cut alternative, no military trade exists with non-neutral nations, meaning total disengagement from major powers in armament. The neutrals would in effect establish a 'Neutral Non-Proliferation Treaty' for *all* types of military supplies. United Neutral military trade would then have become an alternative to international military trade.

We might now dare a final answer to the question whether directed neutral military trade can be a stable alternative to the present neutral armament dilemma. It seems to be a possible alternative in the long run, but for the short term the answer has to be no due to the political, military and structural difficulties involved. For it to be successful, directed trade needs strong and coordinated political planning and support in order to define and conform new

120 Conclusions and Discussion

military demands and to transform the neutral military-industrial structure.

This is no easy task. One prerequisite for the realization of this alternative might even be that steps toward international conventional arms control and disarmament are simultaneously and successfully pursued by other countries. For instance, the then Swedish Minister of Defense declared in November of 1986 that if the European Security Conference discussions resulted in a continuation of the Stockholm Conference with possibilities for conventional arms control, the Swedish government would be prepared to include Swedish forces in such discussions (*Svenska Dagbladet*, November 5, 1986). This takes us to the fourth alternative, which is built upon a successive reduction of armament through neutral cooperation.

Toward Pax Neutralia

Armed neutrality is regarded as a means to increase national security. At the same time, most governments recognize that international arms control and disarmament are necessary for stable and long-term national security. A neutral alternative could opt either to support continued armament and accept the unavoidable effects from that or to support international arms control and disarmament. To seriously, actively and effectively aim for both at the same time seems impossible without serious questioning of the credibility and legitimacy of neutral foreign policy. A change of direction toward the explicit and primary support of international arms control and disarmament would be the most extreme but also the most important future change in the neutral role. Neutrality would in this alternative distance itself from traditional policy as an 'in-between' solution to the existence of military alliances. Instead, neutrality would be an active policy with a strong emphasis upon change.

If international arms control and disarmament, as well as other peace-oriented ingredients of neutral foreign policy, become a reality, the paradox is that neutral policies of today accept increasing foreign military sales. In other words, the more peaceful the world becomes, the more foreign military sales are possible from a neutral supplier's perspective. In a developed neutral alternative, this possibility should, of course, not be taken advantage of – if someone else can sell, let him.

An indefinite continuation of neutral armament, if assumed to be possible, is no long-term guarantee of national security. Most nations include foreign policy and diplomacy, international trade and economic assistance in their national security policy. By tradition, military force has been the most important ingredient. But this frame of reference could change. Economic realities as well as other considerations are making themselves felt in most industrial countries. In Switzerland, for instance, the referendum in November of 1989 of whether or not to abolish the Army was important not only for the result – the 35 per cent votes in favor of abolishing the Army were surprisingly high – but for the fact that the referendum was held at all. With the transformations, or rather revolutions, taking place in the Soviet Union and Eastern Europe, the new confidence-building measures accepted at the Stockholm conference in 1986 and the agreement between the United States and the Soviet Union to abolish certain intermediate and medium range nuclear forces, it is difficult to avoid the feeling that major-power relations have reached not only an important but a historic divide. The Soviet Foreign Minister made his historic visit to the NATO Headquarter in December of 1989. How can traditional and convincing 'enemy images' and threat perceptions be kept alive in parallel with present Soviet openness and dramatic changes? During a recent Swedish military maneuver – the first in Sweden since the Stockholm conference – thirty-seven foreign observers from nineteen countries participated. A high Soviet military observer not only commented to journalists on the way the Swedish forces 'fought the war'; he also talked to his Swedish collegues about it (*Dagens Nyheter*, September 17, 1989, p. 7).

The military-political situation in Europe is changing. Conversion or economic adjustment, meaning the transformation of military activities to fulfill civilian needs, has become a debated and controversial policy issue. In a long-term perspective, conversion would be important for the transformation from a military to a non-military neutral role. So far conversion has not been politically supported in any country as a means to solve the economic difficulties in military production and acquisition. If international steps were taken, individual nations might follow. That was, for instance, the startingpoint in a Swedish study presented to the United Nations in 1984 (*In Pursuit of Disarmament* 1984a; 1984b).

Governmental reactions to conversion have in many ways been similar to the implementation of foreign military sales policy, namely, passivity. In Sweden studies have been made since 1974, when the first special study was commissioned by the Swedish Ministry of Defense, to investigate military industrial problems (*Försvarsindustriella problem* 1975; *Säkerhetspolitik och totalförsvar* 1976). The aeronautical sector in particular has been investigated (*Flygindustrikommitténs betänkande* 1978, 1979;

Flygindustridelegationens betänkande 1980). In Austria a conversion study was presented in 1985 (Van der Bellen et al. 1985), but so far with no visible results. In Finland and Switzerland no similar studies have been made.

Neither in the neutrals nor in any other country has there been direct or concrete political support of conversion. It has been left to industry to work out the solutions. But without coordinated planning as well as political direction and support, military industry will follow commercial demands and will continue to produce military supplies as long as there is no other, more profitable alternative. Because military control requirements are no serious hindrance to foreign military sales, producers will export military supplies whenever possible. By such a policy – whether deliberate or not – governments support diversification rather than conversion and, in effect, continued military production, foreign military sales and global armament.

The quantitative data presented here indicate that in general military production accounts for only a small share of industrial production in the neutral countries. The negative impacts from conversion should therefore be relatively limited. They should be possible to handle with planning, coordination and preparation. The interesting aspect of conversion in this alternative is that it could be used to help create a different neutral alternative. The Integration alternative would also enlarge the market for neutral conversion. Integration could be the basis for a neutral role with reduced emphasis upon a traditional military-political frame of reference. In order to ease a transformation of indigenous military production and a successive conversion from military to civilian activities, the neutrals could establish a 'Neutral Conversion Market'. Such a market would increase neutral civilian trade and create a common employment market for people leaving military production. It could be used to create and to integrate civilian rather than military production and trade among the neutrals. Such an alternative would definitely erode the present dilemma between armament and arms control in neutral policy. Armed neutrality as presently understood would be a policy of the past. A strong neutral role in international arms control and disarmament initiatives would then be fully legitimate.

Such a neutral alternative could become an example for other countries by extending public and political awareness and concern for the dilemma among national military production, foreign military sales, international armament and long-term national security. It is, by no means, only a dilemma for neutral countries. The neutral governments could become the legitimate 'spearheads' in international demands for the conversion of 'swords into plowshares'.

This new neutral structure could grow according to a civilian 'domino theory' to include more and more nations from both East and West. Despite the drastic changes in Eastern Europe and the Soviet Union there is no foreseeable dissolution of the two European military alliances. Security alternatives will continue to be important. Individual states could become independent democracies and join the United Neutrals. Eastern European countries could still have, like Finland today, economic ties with the Soviet Union and other Eastern European countries, but they could also have relations with the EC and/or the EFTA. In a long-term perspective with successful economic, social and political reforms within the Soviet Union and Eastern Europe, a controlled disintegration of the former Communist block might not be unrealistic. Recent developments illustrate steps in such a direction. The speaker of the Hungarian Parliament in September of 1989 stated that Hungary might want to become a neutral state. His view was supported by the leader of one of the opposing parliamentary parties (*Upsala Nya Tidning*, September 20, 1989).

Compared to many other outcomes, this may not be a bad future. A common security policy with minimal military force and maximum civilian relations, initially created among a limited number of United Neutrals, could in this way become the seed of a European 'Pax Neutralia'.

Appendix Tables

APPENDIX A
Recipients of Finnish war materiel sales, 1971-1987 (current prices, 1000 FIM)*

Recipients	1971	1972	1973	1974	1975	1976	1977	1978	1979	1980	1981	1982	1983	1984	1985	1986	1987	Total
Afghanistan	0	4	0	0	0	0	0	0	0	0	0	0	0	0	0	0	0	4
Algeria	0	0	112	0	0	0	0	0	0	0	0	0	0	0	0	32	0	144
Antigua/Barbuda	1	1	0	0	0	0	0	0	0	0	0	0	0	0	0	0	0	2
Argentina	12	1	0	0	48	0	0	114	101	91	0	0	0	165	0	64	0	596
Australia	430	732	1332	245	2461	2882	2131	4508	3946	5449	4515	2050	3758	4469	5578	4969	1364	52819
Austria	341	549	695	1197	1570	1238	1631	1683	1400	997	3857	1846	2755	4911	5893	6011	4805	41379
Bahrain	0	30	11	62	97	0	59	0	192	0	32	769	414	21	0	0	0	1687
Belgium	411	346	1568	405	393	1803	1569	629	353	586	747	351	482	470	721	832	1569	13235
Bolivia	11	42	0	0	0	0	0	0	0	0	157	0	0	0	0	0	0	210
Botswana	0	0	0	0	0	0	0	0	0	0	0	0	0	528	244	0	0	772
Brazil	0	0	0	2	0	0	31	22	115	593	1193	1622	195	436	0	63	289	4561
Brunei	0	0	0	0	0	0	0	0	0	0	0	0	0	0	31	0	0	31
Burkina Faso	0	0	0	1	0	0	0	0	0	0	0	0	0	0	0	0	0	1
Bulgaria	21	0	17	0	11	0	0	0	0	0	32	0	51	253	0	0	4354	4739
Cameroon	3	0	0	0	0	0	0	0	0	0	0	0	0	0	0	0	0	3
Canada	324	323	543	794	613	541	1286	1203	1706	691	1970	1052	2660	3702	5180	4105	8212	34905
Chile	0	15	0	0	0	0	0	0	133	30	0	29	0	0	0	0	0	207
Colombia	0	6	6	13	0	0	0	0	947	1184	0	0	26	191	0	0	267	2628
Costa Rica	3	0	0	5	2	0	0	0	0	0	0	0	1173	0	0	0	39	1234
Cuba	5	0	0	0	0	0	0	0	0	0	0	0	0	0	0	0	0	5
Cyprus	7	45	0	0	10	31	0	54	28	225	239	431	211	0	0	0	371	1611
Czechoslovakia	5	26	4	26	0	0	0	0	0	25	0	0	694	0	1415	1688	4651	8575
Denmark	981	1015	1484	1270	1493	1905	1983	2123	1846	3996	3629	1633	3273	3307	3316	3953	4873	42080
Ecuador	0	0	0	0	0	0	0	0	0	0	0	0	0	520	35	342	135	1032
Egypt	0	1	0	0	0	0	0	0	0	0	0	0	138	0	0	45	0	184
Ethiopia	1	0	0	0	0	0	0	0	0	0	0	0	0	0	0	0	0	1
Fed. Rep. of Germany	1830	2661	3114	2764	5218	6744	5827	5747	8300	7876	12407	7039	8896	9439	9415	15951	10840	124068
France	879	860	1193	1581	2193	2783	5951	2281	2511	3926	6044	9228	14528	5869	3595	5763	4302	73487
German Dem. Republic	32	13	1	12	114	52	77	0	0	24	40	459	732	672	279	132	240	2879
Great Britain	1170	1337	1792	2289	2583	2408	2535	945	1620	2218	3906	1214	3667	2048	3585	2940	5243	41500
Greece	5	11	13	64	510	241	243	223	3573	3024	521	2012	10107	4055	1905	8388	3501	38398
Guatemala	0	29	33	16	297	191	101	223	22	735	413	108	0	0	0	0	0	2168
Hong Kong	0	0	0	0	0	0	0	0	0	0	0	0	0	57	69	56	74	256
Hungary	3	0	0	0	0	104	0	362	0	399	860	557	792	950	1505	1978	2145	9655
Iceland	48	38	51	94	65	61	82	57	108	92	83	51	65	56	44	105	132	1232
India	0	0	0	0	0	0	0	0	0	0	0	0	73	32	0	105	30	240
Indonesia	0	0	1	1	0	140	168	2831	2777	4849	476	1675	3284	21201	20693	4642	0	62738
Iran	0	0	0	1592	0	731	1752	909	469	101	0	82	0	0	0	0	0	4986
Iraq	0	0	0	0	2	0	0	0	44	104	30	69	20	31	0	232	0	652
Ireland	8	3	3	15	14	221	121	32	0	0	0	0	0	0	0	0	10	957
Israel	12	7	0	0	0	0	0	0	0	0	0	0	0	0	0	0	0	19
Italy	301	393	631	934	562	5033	1700	5808	1406	2995	2896	3730	1886	726	2655	2048	3905	37609
Ivory Coast	0	0	0	0	0	0	0	0	0	28	0	0	0	0	0	0	0	28
Japan	0	0	0	0	0	0	0	0	0	0	0	0	0	0	0	0	132	132

																		Total
Kenya	0	0	0	0	0	0	0	0	0	0	5775	0	0	0	0	0		5775
Kuwait	0	5	2	0	0	0	0	0	0	0	749	0	873	46	0	136	628	2439
Lebanon	0	3	0	0	0	0	0	0	0	23	0	0	0	0	0	0	0	29
Lesotho	0	0	3	0	0	0	0	0	0	0	0	0	0	24	0	0	0	59
Libya	0	0	0	2	0	0	0	0	0	0	0	0	0	0	20	0	0	179
Malaysia	11	0	0	0	9	194	188	1715	659	1084	809	104	1051	392	568	143		9171
Malta	0	0	0	2	1	54	33	117	29	247	90	837	1232	882	674	953		157
Netherlands	57	117	146	6	49	159	293	160	557	336	473	90	12359	24302	7341	9615		56701
New Zealand	101	214	344	4	207	340	419	160	345	654	263	1113	1232	882	674	953		7793
Nigeria	0	667	0	0	0	0	0	0	0	0	0	263	117	37	0	0		340
Norway	1376	667	1774	2458	3951	4241	6534	7845	8565	7076	9075	6787	8349	8638	8704	11314		98675
Oman	30	0	0	0	0	0	0	0	97	38	97	38	117	37	0	0		319
Pakistan	6	0	0	0	0	0	0	0	0	0	0	0	0	0	0	0		6
Panama	0	0	0	0	0	0	0	0	28	21	28	0	0	0	0	0		49
Peoples Rep. of China	0	3	0	0	0	0	0	0	29	123	29	0	0	0	0	0		347
Peru	0	8	295	776	247	35	517	317	805	624	512	1110	131	934	45	19		8248
Philippines	15	34	0	97	97	3294	0	312	0	0	0	38	411	0	996	948		28
Poland	0	0	0	0	35	71	322	312	815	287	635	521	17177	2186	6907	5		543
Portugal	0	0	123	265	3294	6639	5528	2719	787	1054	1430	1726	154	399	317	4		40986
Qatar	0	0	0	65	24	71	0	43	0	60	889	0	0	0	0	11558		21612
Rumania	6	8	121	43	0	0	0	0	0	0	97	38	154	399	317	19		381
Saudi Arabia	1585	2013	2570	3102	2436	3272	2157	2134	2430	4933	20202	21058	22171	25324	7523	62		950
Singapore	0	0	0	6370	2436	3272	2157	2134	104	51	78	189	32	480	350	118		129342
South Africa	0	0	0	0	0	0	0	0	0	0	0	0	0	0	0	0		2
South Korea	13	54	170	36	28	1042	2719	1388	628	413	1268	682	407	182	291	742		1473
Soviet Union	117	201	318	377	1871	1479	979	682	2548	1827	1154	270	632	619	994	2080		10065
Spain	105	318	377	1599	1871	1479	979	682	52	0	52	0	0	0	0	0		17747
Sudan	0	0	14	0	0	0	0	0	0	0	0	0	0	0	0	0		171
Surinam	1	10	0	0	0	0	0	0	0	0	103	0	372	0	0	4		10
Swaziland	0	0	0	0	0	0	0	0	0	0	0	0	0	0	0	0		1
Sweden	5754	4576	4311	13581	19459	21123	15503	21603	25287	28444	23798	23487	29777	31468	29600	26324		328997
Switzerland	58	69	111	296	164	391	753	387	2952	635	1819	2754	1686	1985	1336	1628		17224
Tanzania	13	5	0	2	0	0	0	0	140	0	110	0	72	36	32	18		176
Thailand	156	885	72	39	37	39	0	25	220	422	2033	972	830	8353	41	838		14964
Trinidad/Tobago	0	0	0	0	0	0	0	0	0	0	0	0	0	0	0	6		6
Tunisia	0	0	0	0	0	0	0	0	0	0	49	0	0	0	0	0		49
Turkey	0	0	0	0	0	0	0	0	103	0	103	0	372	0	647	89		1211
United States	7153	8736	8450	10955	10470	6227	4835	5780	11936	8958	13138	10931	18558	23269	27686	20982		206924
Uruguay	7	0	1	0	140	224	214	41	892	20	137	83	37	141	25	59		1435
Venezuela	23	2	15	50	0	179	1123	151	140	811	110	981	26	1448	773	110		1747
Yugoslavia	1	14	0	0	0	0	0	0	1376	0	1005	0	0	0	1507	3936		12620
Zambia	0	0	0	0	0	0	0	0	0	0	79	0	42	0	0	2		82
Zimbabwe	0	0	0	0	0	0	0	0	0	0	579	0	42	0	161	236		1018
Other	0	0	0	1	0	4	4	10	51	5	13	32	12	1	0	0		132
Totals	23432	26121	30699	35237	55075	70016	73442	73013	73720	98083	105296	133914	195266	182655	161118	153923		1613837

* Customs authorities. Figures supplied by Pertti Joenniemi.

APPENDIX B
Recipients of Swedish war materiel sales, 1971-1988 (current prices, 1000 SEK)*

Recipients	1971**	1972	1973	1974	1975	1976	1977	1978	1979
Albania	0	0	0	0	0	0	0	0	750
Algeria	0	0	0	0	15	0	0	0	0
Andorra	-	-	-	-	0	0	0	12	0
Argentina	35	100	87	2115	345	29	291	259	32
Australia	351	312	549	484	566	3047	223	337	2989
Austria	97004	65782	5084	5997	14042	19268	38052	15326	17673
Bangladesh	0	0	0	0	0	0	0	0	0
Barbados	0	0	0	0	0	0	0	0	0
Belgium	1729	1026	624	4501	3062	3591	2900	8245	14500
Brasil	0	0	0	0	1	945	11204	1036	769
Brunei	0	0	0	335	0	0	0	0	0
Bulgaria	0	0	0	0	0	0	0	0	0
Burma (Myanmar)	321	8	21	0	0	0	31	0	0
Cameroon	0	0	0	0	0	0	0	0	0
Canada	9665	4382	5395	1690	5921	9889	27479	3800	18335
Chile	38898	284	1040	9	0	0	0	0	0
Colombia	806	363	701	66	0	0	0	0	0
Czechoslovakia	0	0	0	0	0	108	55	90	99
Denmark	256361	36955	35389	33961	56817	145362	75931	41140	60637
Ecuador	7	0	0	0	0	0	0	0	0
Egypt	0	0	0	0	0	0	0	0	0
Fed. Rep. of Germany	17135	13114	24602	34602	15886	17320	26371	38493	48722
Finland	1690	19361	92502	146814	68931	32813	45919	35381	27566
France	1161	1685	379	1891	938	1944	4543	12647	26839
Gabon	-	-	-	-	0	0	0	0	0
German Dem. Republic	0	0	0	0	0	0	0	85	56
Ghana	0	0	0	0	2794	5277	726	0	0
Gibraltar	-	-	-	-	-	6	4	0	0
Great Britain	24821	20619	19493	27422	54202	43797	43161	45876	175037
Greece	0	0	0	0	0	0	0	0	17
Guyana	5	0	0	0	0	0	0	0	0
Hong Kong	0	0	0	0	0	0	0	0	0
Hungary	27	15	13	18	51	26	17	20	5
Iceland	0	4	5	2	2	1	5	0	14
India	40809	37250	13377	23083	52666	14205	28261	64182	61062
Indonesia	13	0	0	0	0	458	494	38205	72150
Iran	0	2921	3669	2736	14981	18166	41824	21934	1457
Ireland	107	1143	406	194	1237	1267	1974	2835	12576
Italy	2886	7907	15895	7687	10035	18175	36684	61609	130902
Japan	1497	2226	1110	2604	1378	677	1000	1209	9846
Luxemburg	17	8	13	23	24	17	34	16	87
Malaysia	4135	12558	5358	8140	19011	10310	86366	98734	333743
Martinique	0	0	0	0	0	0	13	2	0
Mauritius	0	0	0	0	0	0	0	0	0
Mexico	0	0	0	0	0	0	0	0	0
Nepal	0	0	0	0	0	0	0	0	0
Netherlands	5247	2403	2253	1581	2597	7034	8198	73306	109801
New Caledonia	0	0	0	0	12	20	0	0	19
New Zealand	200	201	225	296	400	106	106	84	123
Nigeria	0	0	0	0	33092	2228	0	28860	13196
Norway	28203	51447	43936	58827	58846	44248	61245	64162	69312
Pakistan	5516	2401	3538	1108	7782	10813	1268	3434	1648
Peru	0	0	0	0	0	0	0	8072	29361
Philippines	0	0	16	0	0	0	0	0	0
Poland	0	0	0	0	66	26	0	21	88
Portugal	594	1061	60	96	0	0	0	0	0
Rumania	0	0	0	0	0	0	0	0	0
Singapore	2933	17191	15924	24521	10147	18686	12851	1979	166365
Spain	0	0	28	337	131	40	266	52	7380
Sri Lanka	0	0	0	0	0	0	0	0	0
Surinam	0	0	0	0	0	0	0	31831	0
Swizerland	81601	48619	32172	33168	65223	44160	83211	105396	27618
Tanzania	-	-	8	0	0	0	0	0	0
Thailand	21	45	107	0	0	15	0	0	0
Togo	0	0	0	0	0	0	6	9	0
Trinidad/Tobago	0	0	0	0	0	0	0	0	0
Tunisia	0	0	0	0	0	0	0	0	0
Turkey	5	0	0	0	0	0	0	0	0
United States	2597	5846	5319	4550	8207	6357	7976	18106	20810
Uruguay	0	0	0	0	0	0	0	0	0
Venezuela	-	1594	1344	2868	1550	2124	1422	3081	0
Yugoslavia	236	73	4420	43849	23667	19798	45255	75255	209640
Totals	626633	358904	335062	475575	534625	502366	695355	905119	1671224

1980	1981	1982	1983	1984	1985	1986	1987	1988	Totals
2250	1125	2735	524	0	0	0	0	0	7384
200	0	0	0	0	0	0	0	0	215
0	0	20	0	0	0	0	0	0	32
185	0	0	0	35255	35494	6	15643	39049	128925
21362	11209	27837	13983	26848	32211	88154	14148	20812	265422
37064	51368	39358	43305	75671	28200	64238	367740	393073	1378245
0	0	0	0	0	11188	35764	571	0	47523
0	0	0	0	60	0	0	0	0	60
4740	3822	5785	13512	1855	2695	4218	2999	2843	82647
589	6233	1182	1367	44941	89088	276215	92958	87862	614390
0	0	0	0	0	0	0	0	0	335
0	0	0	0	1673	0	0	0	0	1673
286	0	0	33038	0	0	0	0	0	33705
0	0	13237	8631	0	0	0	0	0	21868
590	643	33217	45229	32310	74773	39472	170404	36686	519880
0	0	0	0	0	0	0	0	0	40231
345	0	0	0	0	0	0	0	0	2281
0	0	8	4	0	86	16	57	0	523
56916	54166	62718	79348	85045	86739	199253	181593	135632	1683963
0	0	0	0	49102	0	0	0	0	49109
0	0	0	0	0	0	0	0	67	67
86424	119664	71759	101330	55120	29376	59310	153358	327717	1240303
44387	57014	50446	53393	108840	335623	514607	296846	73129	2005262
10017	17823	31250	52497	24927	4050	3494	5868	6192	208145
0	2223	0	0	6330	0	0	19442	260	28255
466	20	47	6	8	91	71	48	58	956
11500	2910	0	0	0	1250	117	0	0	24574
0	0	0	0	0	0	0	0	0	10
75414	188073	112151	64820	182112	112418	46120	52955	11826	1300317
1	5531	3270	7261	564	23053	780	2226	70303	113006
0	0	0	0	0	0	0	0	0	5
4	0	582	0	34	169	861	518	188	2356
36	38	0	4	0	5	0	3	14	292
21	90	102	52	75	20	49	34	111	587
53076	133836	52204	131900	53986	77528	312215	1387410	2833205	5370255
26410	44831	92494	24728	69072	26798	104409	51269	17756	569087
1	0	0	0	0	0	0	0	0	107689
15112	11263	2322	16026	13103	5244	16693	10280	3582	115364
73584	63721	50466	159266	298325	18177	158080	86870	65704	1265973
12298	32241	36008	44143	39085	37074	10835	16156	6819	256206
72	54	86	97	48	0	0	0	0	596
261893	268347	122978	100157	63742	106138	81771	40621	29234	1653236
0	0	0	0	0	0	0	0	0	15
0	0	9	26	0	0	0	0	0	35
0	0	51929	2013	0	0	0	39495	10673	104110
0	0	0	0	0	10998	0	0	0	10998
24300	9565	20778	10495	12975	22308	13413	41668	101370	469292
80	0	92	48	15	0	0	0	0	286
242	402	736	584	596	3183	1518	1060	8756	18818
24023	6595	89198	196769	293740	94962	10325	28045	28370	849403
175227	163116	70660	60888	135801	251908	457513	519958	644475	2959772
1491	1501	2020	48716	6545	4030	239418	185762	75923	602914
17865	385	1080	32361	113	19390	3607	4999	0	117233
0	0	0	0	0	0	0	0	0	16
0	0	0	0	0	0	0	0	0	201
0	4542	3722	4512	4719	372	100	125	1215	21118
7511	0	1900	0	285	710	0	0	0	10406
205994	83250	198426	122417	187926	307516	251581	31172	82628	1741507
20882	16455	3060	239	34707	2039	1424	7269	2044	96353
0	0	1925	0	0	0	0	0	0	1925
0	0	0	0	0	0	0	0	0	31831
140692	161475	141011	83987	16436	69780	90996	69811	113599	1408955
0	0	0	0	0	0	0	0	0	8
0	0	0	0	0	0	0	0	0	188
0	0	0	0	0	0	0	0	0	15
101152	0	0	0	0	0	0	0	0	101152
169774	16859	0	309	16023	0	134	23235	867	227201
0	0	0	0	0	0	0	0	0	5
18122	22909	38194	62238	123641	92395	87447	441325	631339	1597378
0	0	0	0	0	0	26	2	0	28
0	0	218	0	36916	35112	0	0	210839	297068
375463	133744	150475	37952	39357	85164	68686	62652	80227	1455913
2078061	1697043	1587695	1658175	2177926	2137355	3242935	4426595	6154448	31265096

* Figures from War Materiels Inspectorate annual reports.

** The years 1971 to 1975 are not completely comparable with later years because the Defense Materiel Administration and other war materiel exporters were not included.

APPENDIX C
Recipients of Swiss war materiel sales, 1971-1988 (current prices, 1000 SFr)*

Recipients	1971	1972	1973	1974	1975	1976	1977	1978	1979
Algeria	0	0	20	390	1099	903	1267	549	404
Argentina	6130	158	0	0	0	0	95	481	645
Austria	5664	8383	18843	66842	10078	40247	45985	37919	67461
Bahrain	0	0	0	0	0	0	0	0	0
Belgium/Luxemburg	81	3849	1979	248	235	280	2012	2139	3954
Bolivia	2928	1060	1927	0	0	0	0	0	0
Brazil	0	0	0	0	5142	24	3643	0	15
Brunei	0	0	0	0	0	204	236	224	40
Burma (Myanmar)	0	0	0	0	0	0	0	0	0
Canada	0	1	88	9	39	29	1032	6575	32
Chile	7151	4072	3881	0	0	0	0	32	0
Colombia	0	0	0	5	0	0	0	69	0
Denmark	48	23	6	0	50	38	1203	1562	2429
Dubai/UAE	0	0	0	0	0	0	0	0	19
Ecuador	1198	0	0	0	0	0	4576	0	15493
Egypt	-	-	-	-	-	-	-	-	-
Fed. Rep. of Germany	47134	50019	35710	18911	87806	124393	216346	127941	141823
Finland	55	21	98	173	94	214	230	159	273
France	1125	2305	2233	944	2883	1582	3208	2310	3162
Ghana	0	0	0	0	0	8718	33370	30390	0
Great Britain	795	3783	3047	2797	6359	2296	699	4033	2197
Greece	1370	608	577	487	3126	2132	335	488	276
India	0	0	0	0	0	0	0	0	0
Indonesia	0	0	0	277	0	16	0	49	0
Iran	54718	92035	91026	52118	118799	114697	19425	8977	0
Italy	3166	1471	2165	2053	8492	9043	31239	38512	24923
Japan	13377	9020	5205	332	168	83	42	164	2329
Kamaran	0	0	0	0	0	0	0	0	0
Kuwait	0	0	0	0	0	0	0	0	0
Liberia	0	0	0	0	0	0	0	0	0
Malaysia	0	0	1733	274	115	1566	0	12	0
Mexico	0	0	2175	2682	0	0	0	0	0
Morocco	0	0	0	0	103	542	518	199	144
Netherlands	7202	1522	1821	3192	6529	58818	51903	54077	54357
Nigeria	0	0	0	0	0	0	0	0	0
Norway	1179	4887	3688	2082	14910	7528	1791	774	2673
Oman	0	0	0	0	0	0	0	0	0
Pakistan	0	0	0	0	0	0	0	0	0
Philippines	0	0	0	0	15	0	0	0	5557
Peoples Rep. of China	0	0	0	0	0	0	0	0	0
Peru	2646	338	222	1162	1340	2102	1419	785	1729
Portugal	19	215	329	448	421	155	588	354	334
Qatar	0	0	0	0	0	0	0	0	0
Saudi Arabia	0	0	0	0	0	0	11	0	24
Sierra Leone	2047	0	0	0	0	0	0	0	0
Singapore	21759	8190	1548	57	3054	630	21159	1112	8123
South Africa	0	0	0	0	0	0	0	0	32
Spain	3549	2859	25690	49822	88142	100973	55074	80431	55276
Sweden	4656	6273	3912	4966	8983	11890	14749	21320	27247
Taiwan	-	-	-	-	-	-	-	-	-
Thailand	0	0	0	0	24	133	21	19	0
Tunisia	0	0	0	0	0	331	131	265	0
Turkey	0	0	0	11	0	12	0	0	0
United States	254	3012	3009	1887	596	1714	851	3470	3747
Venezuela	0	0	0	0	16	238	0	23	44
Yugoslavia	0	0	0	13	55	30	19	123	79
Other	110	107	124	270	135	163	216	262	266
Totals	188361	204211	211056	212452	368808	491724	513393	425799	425107

1980	1981	1982	1983	1984	1985	1986	1987	1988	Totals
2789	919	1984	1687	1188	1771	1675	1456	1060	19161
1191	1698	47	0	1	2528	96	110	460	13640
22160	76109	67993	71028	27753	14879	20455	42251	31443	675493
0	0	0	0	18733	28663	2607	28529	1121	79653
25848	4992	8311	19485	21943	1663	4293	1298	1790	104400
0	0	0	0	0	0	0	0	0	5915
40	0	0	526	536	6637	5615	8475	5537	36190
18	40	8	0	75	15	17	44	108	1029
0	0	0	0	10	154	2	0	0	166
21	163	4445	528	1154	325	5516	377	27015	47349
0	0	0	0	0	1	13	0	1	15151
29	258	300	210	2	136	572	300	70	1951
2149	2282	2674	2568	2496	3353	2559	1883	2123	27446
0	53	69	2878	23315	6958	1068	1215	4799	40374
10077	0	16	5641	246	658	771	9850	4209	52735
-	-	-	-	-	-	-	-	-	256
118304	143733	96652	60564	57322	16008	62474	89820	79710	1574670
3208	620	834	1272	1483	855	1978	595	10525	22687
3299	6846	8770	8230	5914	5386	3676	4325	3271	69469
0	0	0	0	0	0	0	2	0	72480
5222	2034	10031	14712	32224	10314	8387	19554	17239	145723
1120	30178	98613	15255	67341	35924	1369	1196	1354	261749
172	27	106	261	97	158	95	1208	203	2327
0	0	289	9	683	62	3	258	0	1646
0	0	0	0	0	0	0	0	0	551795
16831	2895	3667	17393	38477	24680	25596	21969	11187	283759
450	2497	793	2858	1856	4655	168	3345	12757	60099
0	0	0	1	594	38	0	15	0	648
0	0	15	13	39	3	23	2	2	97
0	0	2809	0	0	0	0	147	0	2956
734	0	1	4448	5850	4998	6092	214	79	26116
28	0	0	2	0	6	0	0	2	4895
525	476	612	574	761	899	535	404	509	6801
29537	8311	8113	43789	8416	6908	13904	16127	13957	388483
0	149969	87882	59310	0	83664	80754	30	105820	567429
494	392	418	447	437	911	941	839	708	45099
0	106	144	110	0	378	510	0	46	1294
0	0	0	68	2	104	32105	2491	18885	53655
0	2363	0	2	4	0	0	3	45	7989
0	0	0	0	600	311	0	0	0	911
3386	1236	408	580	667	646	532	0	155	19353
774	532	474	531	365	326	334	425	683	7307
0	0	0	0	14	48	0	0	1737	1799
28	38	24	15	20061	101110	32616	177581	59122	390630
2419	0	0	0	0	0	0	0	0	4466
8623	9632	4717	1976	1895	7790	19638	15409	9514	144826
0	156	297	307	102	133	4	238	195	1464
25802	17724	9871	6394	5773	11483	7035	2130	1637	549665
51386	44555	36697	23674	18886	18219	16842	27034	17157	358446
-	-	-	-	-	-	-	-	55	55
0	0	0	16	74	424	124	300	20196	21331
1214	0	0	0	0	0	0	5	2	1948
0	38	9191	4123	439	118880	111639	64431	8114	316878
2367	342	3913	5416	15877	17147	15304	29830	26981	135717
22	14	22	1	8141	0	8	727	1519	10775
50	68	34	172	315	105	316	1709	859	3947
286	238	59	162	171	315	244	108	177	3413
340603	511534	471303	377236	392332	540629	488505	578259	504394	7245706

* Monthly foreign trade statistics. 1971-1974: explosives (2903.10, 2907.10, 2918.10, 2922.20, 2926.20, 3601.01, 3602.01, 3604.01, 3603.01), armored vehicles (8708.01), weapons (9303.01), munitions (9307.10/20, 9306.20). 1975-1988: Monthly statistical compilations published by the customs authorities. Figures supplied by Peter Hug.

132

APPENDIX D, continued

Africa	
Northwest	Algeria (F, Swe, Swi)
	Morocco (Swi)
East	Ethiopia (F)
	Kenya (F)
Southern	Botswana (F)
	Lesotho (F)
	S. Africa (F, Swi)
	Swaziland (F)
	Tanzania (F, Swe)
	Zambia (F)
Other	Burkina Faso (F)
	Cameroon (F, Swe)
	Gabon (Swe)
	Ghana (Swe, Swi)
	Ivory Coast (F)
	Liberia (Swi)
	Kamaran (Swi)
	Libya (F)
	Nigeria (F, Swe, Swi)
	Sierra Leone (Swi)
	Sudan (F)
	Togo (Swe)
	Tunisia (F, Swe, Swi)
	Zimbabwe (F)

Asia	
South	Afghanistan (F)
	Bangladesh (Swe)
	India (F, Swe, Swi)
	Nepal (Swe)
	Pakistan (F, Swe, Swi)
	Sri Lanka (Swe)
Southeast	Brunei (F, Swe, Swi)
	Burma/Myanmar (Swe, Swi)
	Indonesia (F, Swe, Swi)
	Malaysia (F, Swe, Swi)
	Singapore (F, Swe, Swi)
	Thailand (F, Swe, Swi)
Other	Australia (F, Swe)
	Hong Kong (F, Swe)
	Japan (F, Swe, Swi)
	Mauritius (Swe)
	New Caledonia (Swe)
	New Zealand (F, Swe)
	P. Rep. of China (F, Swi)
	Philippines (F, Swe, Swi)
	South Korea (F)

* Suppliers: F=Finland, Swe=Sweden, Swi=Switzerland

APPENDIX D, continued

Africa	
Northwest	Algeria (F, Swe, Swi) Morocco (Swi)
East	Ethiopia (F) Kenya (F)
Southern	Botswana (F) Lesotho (F) S. Africa (F, Swi) Swaziland (F) Tanzania (F, Swe) Zambia (F)
Other	Burkina Faso (F) Cameroon (F, Swe) Gabon (Swe) Ghana (Swe, Swi) Ivory Coast (F) Liberia (Swi) Kamaran (Swi) Libya (F) Nigeria (F, Swe, Swi) Sierra Leone (Swi) Sudan (F) Togo (Swe) Tunisia (F, Swe, Swi) Zimbabwe (F)

Asia	
South	Afghanistan (F) Bangladesh (Swe) India (F, Swe, Swi) Nepal (Swe) Pakistan (F, Swe, Swi) Sri Lanka (Swe)
Southeast	Brunei (F, Swe, Swi) Burma/Myanma (Swe, Swi) Indonesia (F, Swe, Swi) Malaysia (F, Swe, Swi) Singapore (F, Swe, Swi) Thailand (F, Swe, Swi)
Other	Australia (F, Swe) Hong Kong (F, Swe) Japan (F, Swe, Swi) Mauritius (Swe) New Caledonia (Swe) New Zealand (F, Swe) P. Rep. of China (F, Swi) Philippines (F, Swe, Swi) South Korea (F)

* Suppliers: F=Finland, Swe=Sweden, Swi=Switzerland

Bibliography

Agrell, Wilhelm. 1981. *Rustningens Drivkrafter*. Lund: Studentlitteratur.

————. 1984. *Sveriges Civila Säkerhet*. Stockholm: Liber Förlag.

————. 1985. *Alliansfrihet och Atombomber*. Stockholm: Liber Förlag.

————. 1986. *Ubåtshotet*. Stockholm: Liber Förlag.

————. 1989. *Vetenskapen i Försvarets Tjänst*. Lund: Lund University Press.

Albrecht, Ulrich. 1988. The role of neutral and non-aligned countries in a world of global powers. *Current Research on Peace and Violence*, no. 3.

Albrecht, Ulrich et al. 1978. *A Short Research Guide on Arms and Armed Forces*. London: Croom Helm.

Albrecht, Ulrich et al. 1988. Neutrality: The need for conceptual revision. *Occasional Papers*, no. 35. Tampere: Tampere Peace Research Institute.

Allison, Roy. 1985. *Finland's Relations with the Soviet Union 1944-84*. Oxford: Macmillan.

Andersson, Bo, & Bjarne Stenquist. 1988. *Vapensmugglarna*. Stockholm: Författarförlaget.

Andrén, Nils (ed.). 1984. *Säkerhetspolitik i Norden*. Stockholm: Folk och Försvar.

Anförande. 1988. Statsminister Ingvar Carlsson. *Svensk krigsmaterielexport*. Stockholm: Ministry of Foreign Affairs.

Armed Forces Journal International. Monthly. Washington, D.C.

The Arms Trade with the Third World. 1971. Uppsala: Almqvist & Wiksell.

Artéus, Gunnar. 1982. Svensk Militärhistorisk Forskning under 1900-talet. Stockholm: Militärhistoriska Förlaget.

Åström, Sverker. 1977. Sweden's Policy of Neutrality. Stockholm: Swedish Institute.

Austria. 1987. Neutrals in Europe. Conference papers, no. 7. Stockholm: Institute for Foreign Affairs.

Aviation Week and Space Technology. Weekly. New York.

Axelrod, Robert. 1980. The Evolution of Cooperation. New York: Basic Books.

Azar, Edward, & John Burton (eds.). 1986. International Conflict Resolution. Brighton: Wheatsheaf.

B3LA-beredningens rapport. 1977. Report DsFö 1977, no. 7. Stockholm: Ministry of Defense.

Bajusz, William, & David Louscher. 1988. Arms Sales and the U.S. Economy: The Impact of Restricting Military Exports. Boulder, Colo.: Westview.

Ball, Nicole. 1985. Conversion outside Sweden. In Pursuit of Disarmament. 1985, ch. 2.

Ball, Nicole, & Milton Leitenberg (eds.). 1983. The Structure of the Defense Industry. London: Croom Helm.

Bergom-Larsson, Maria (ed.). 1979. Rusta för Fred, Rädda Livet. Stockholm: Gidlunds Förlag.

Bericht der bundesregierung zu entschliessungen des nationalrates betreffend kriegsmaterial. 1985. Appendix to protokoll. XVII Gesetzgebungsperiode. Bern: Nationalrates.

Berner, Örjan. 1985. Sovjet och Norden. Stockholm: BonnierFakta.

Berry, Nicholas. 1989. Foreign policy and the press. Report presented at the International Studies Association Conference, London, March 28-April 1.

Betänkande med förslag till viss utvidgad statlig kontroll å krigsmaterielområdet. 1959. Stockholm: Ministry of Trade (War Materiel Inspectorate).

Blackaby, Frank, & Thomas Ohlson. 1982. Military expenditure and arms trade: Problems of data. *Bulletin of Peace Proposals* 13, no. 4.

Blainey, Geoffrey. 1973. *The Causes of War.* New York: Free Press.

Boforskanonen i Andra Världskriget. 1961. Försvarsstabens krigshistoriska avdelning. Stockholm: Fröléen & Co.

Boulding, Kenneth. 1982. *Conflict and Defense.* New York: Harper & Row.

Boulton, David. 1978. *The Grease Machine.* Hagerstown: Harper & Row.

Bratt, Ingvar. 1988. *Mot Rädslan.* Stockholm: Carlssons Förlag.

Brogan, Patrick, & Albert Zarca. 1983. *Deadly Business: Sam Cummings, Interarms and the Arms Trade.* New York: Norton.

Brzoska, Michael. 1982. Arms transfer data sources. *Journal of Conflict Resolution* 26, no. 1. March.

Brzoska, Michael, & Thomas Ohlson. 1987. *Arms Transfers to the Third World 1971-1985.* Oxford: Oxford University Press.

Burton, John. 1980. Europe's neutral states' impact on global arms market. *Strategy Week* 6, no. 23. June 2-8.

Carlberg, Ingrid. 1989. *Svenska företag som politiska påtryckare.* Maktutredningen. Uppsala: Uppsala University.

Catrina, Christian. 1988. *Arms Transfers and Dependence.* United Nations Institute for Disarmament Research. New York: Taylor & Francis.

CH-Landesverteidigung. 1987. Internationale Vergleiche. Bern: Stab der Gruppe für Generalstabsdienste. May.

Challenges and Responses in European Security. 1986. Tampere: Tampere Peace Research Institute.

Civil produktion i försvarsindustrin. 1982. Report DsI 1982, no. 1. Stockholm: Ministry of Industry.

Civil produktion i försvarsindustrin genom teknikupphandling. 1983. Report DsI 1983, no. 1. Stockholm: Ministry of Industry.

Clarke, John. 1982. NATO, neutrals and national defence. *Survival* 24, no. 6.

Close up Austria. 1983. *Military Technology* (special supplement) 7, no. 7.

Cooling, Benjamin Franklin (ed.). 1981. *War, Business and World Military-Industrial Complexes.* A National University publication. New York: Kennikat Press.

Dagens Industri. 20 nos./month. Stockholm.

Dagens Nyheter. Daily. Stockholm.

Danckwardt, Jean-Carlos, & Sven Hellman. 1966. *Svensk säkerhetspolitik.* Report SOU 1966, no. 56. Stockholm: Ministry of Defense.

Däniker, Gustav. 1986. *The Swiss model of conventional defense.* Bern: Staff for Strategic and Operational Training. April.

Davidsson, Sune. 1976. *Sveriges Utlandsberoende.* Stockholm: Folk och Försvar.

Defence equipment from Finland. 1988. Helsinki: Foreign Trade Association.

Defense & Armaments Heracles International. Monthly. Paris.

Defense & Foreign Affairs Handbook. Annual. London: Copley & Associates.

Documents on Swedish Foreign Policy. Annual. Stockholm: Ministry of Foreign Affairs.

Dörfer, Ingmar. 1973. *System 37 Viggen.* Oslo: Universitetsforlaget.

--------. 1983. *Arms Deal.* New York: Praeger.

En politik för nedrustning och utveckling. 1988. Stockholm: Ministry of Foreign Affairs.

Elva Åsikter om Svensk Säkerhetspolitik. 1979. Stockholm: Folk och Försvar.

Erlander, Tage. 1976. *1955-1960.* Stockholm: Tidens Förlag.

Everts, Philip. 1989. *The peace movement and public opinion.* Paper presented at the International Studies Association Conference, London, March 28-April 1.

Executive Sessions of the Senate Foreign Relations Committee. 1984. Historical series 13, part 2. 87th Cong., 1st sess. 1961. Washington, D.C.: Committee on Foreign Relations.

Export of Strategic Materials to the USSR and Other Soviet Bloc Countries. 1961. Hearing before the subcommittee to investigate the administration of the International Security Act and other international security laws of the Committee on the Judiciary, 87th Cong., 1st sess., part 2. Washington, D.C.: U.S. Senate. October 24.

Farley, Philip. et al. 1978. *Arms Across the Sea.* Washington, D.C.: Brookings Institution.

FFV, Förenade Fabriksverken. 1974. Report SOU 1974, no. 38. Betänkande av 1972 års FFV-utredning. Stockholm: Ministry of Industry.

FFV-nytt. Irregular. Eskilstuna.

Finland. 1984. Länder i fickformat. Stockholm: Institute for Foreign Affairs.

Flight International. Weekly. London.

Flyghistorisk Revy. Stockholm (Swedish Aviation Historical Society).

Flygindustridelegationens betänkande. 1980. Report DsI 1980, no. 2. Stockholm: Ministry of Industry.

Flygindustrikommitténs betänkande. 1978. Part 1. Report DsFö 1978, no. 8. Stockholm: Ministry of Defense.

Flygindustrikommitténs betänkande. 1979. Part 2. Report DsFö 1979, no. 1. Stockholm: Ministry of Defense.

Flygtekniska Försöksanstalten. 1967. Report 1967, no. 6. Stockholm: Ministry of Defense. Mimeographed.

FMV-Aktuellt. 4-6 nos./year. Stockholm: Defense Materiel Administration.

FMV report. Annual. Stockholm: Defense Materiel Administration.

Fogelström, Per Anders. 1971. *Kampen för Fred.* Stockholm: Bonniers.

Folk och Försvar. 4 nos./year. Stockholm.

Föreskrifter och anvisningar för tillverkare och försäljare av krigsmateriel. 1972. Stockholm: Ministry of Trade (War Materiel Inspectorate).

Forskning, industri och säkerhetspolitik för 1990-talet. 1985. Report no. 299. Stockholm: Ingenjörsvetenskapsakademien.

140 Bibliography

Forskning och utveckling i utlandet. 1989. Report IVA-PM, no. 1. Stockholm: Ingenjörsvetenskapsakademien.

Forskningsstatistik. Annual. Stockholm: Central Bureau of Statistics.

Försvaret och den tekniska utvecklingen. 1977. Report no. 97. Stockholm: Ingenjörsvetenskapsakademien.

Försvarsindustriella problem. 1975. Stockholm: Ministry of Defense.

Försvarsindustrins utlandsverksamhet. 1987. Report SOU 1987, no. 8. Stockholm: Ministry of Foreign Affairs.

Försvarsstatistik. Annual. Stockholm: Ministry of Defense.

Försvarstjänstemannen. 10 nos./year. Stockholm (Civilian defense employees).

Framtida militär flygindustri i Sverige. 1981. Report DsFö 1981, no. 2. Stockholm: Ministry of Defense.

Fredspolitik för 90-talet. 1989. Stockholm: Svenska Ekumeniska Nämnden.

Frei, Daniel. 1983. *Swiss Foreign Policy.* Swiss Council for the Arts. Zürich: Pro Helvetia.

Friedenspolitik. 1-2 nos./month. Basel.

Friedenszeitung. Monthly. Zürich.

Galtung, Johan. 1967. *Fredsforskning.* Stockholm: Prisma.

--------. 1975. *Är Fred Möjlig?* Stockholm: Prisma.

General defense. 1976. Report of the Federal Council to the Federal Assembly on the security policy of Switzerland. Bern: Zentralstelle für Gesamtverteidigung. August.

Goldmann, Kjell et al. 1985. *Democracy and Foreign Policy: The Case of Sweden.* Aldershot: Gower.

Greenwood, Ted. 1975. *Making the MIRV: A Study of Defense Decision Making.* Cambridge, Mass.: Ballinger.

Gunston, Bill. 1976. *Early Supersonic Fighters of the West.* London: Ian Allan.

Gunther, John. 1961. *Inside Europe today.* New York: Harper & Brothers.

Hagelin, Björn. 1977. *Militärindustriellt Samarbete i Västeuropa*. Stockholm: Folk och Försvar.

--------. 1978. International cooperation in conventional weapons acquisition: A threat to armament control? *Bulletin of Peace Proposals* 9, no. 2.

--------. 1979. I vilka händer, när det händer? Bergom-Larsson (1979)

--------. 1981. Svensk militär export – eller hur man rymmer ett isberg i ett äggskal. *Internationella Studier*, no. 5. Stockholm: Institute for Foreign Affairs.

--------. 1983. Ett svenskt militärindustri-politiskt brödraskap? *Internationella Studier*, no. 5. Stockholm: Institute for Foreign Affairs.

--------. 1984. Multinational weapon projects and international arms trade. *World Armaments and Disarmament*.

--------. 1985. *Kulorna Rullar*. Stockholm: Ordfront Förlag.

--------. 1986. Nordic armaments and military dependencies. *Current Research on Peace and Violence* 9, nos. 1-2. Tampere: Tampere Peace Research Institute.

--------. 1988. Arms transfer limitations: The case of Sweden. Ohlson (1988).

Hakovirta, Harto. 1988. *East-West Conflict and European Neutrality*. Oxford: Oxford University Press.

--------. 1989. *Borrowed force in Finland's security and defence - the military mechanisms of the Finnish-Soviet 1948 treaty*. Paper presented at the International Studies Association Conference, London, March 28-April 1.

Halperin, Morton. 1974. *Bureaucratic Politics and Foreign Policy*. Washington, D.C.: Brookings Institution.

Handbok i Finlands Säkerhetspolitik. 1984. Publication no. 1. Helsingfors: Planeringskommissionen för Försvarsinformation.

Harkavy, Robert. 1975. *The Arms Trade and International Systems*. Cambridge, Mass.: Ballinger.

Harle, Vilho. 1977. *The aircraft purchases by the Finnish Air Force 1970-1976*. Paper presented at symposium, Berlin, May 19-20. Mimeographed.

Harle, Vilho (ed.). 1986. *Challenges and Responses in European Security*. Aldershot: Avebury.

Hellman, Sven. 1976. *Säkerhetspolitik och försvarsindustri*. Report SSLP, no. 9. Stockholm: Ministry of Defense.

Herlitz, C. (ed.). 1980. *Luftvärnets Historia*, Stockholm: Militärhistoriska Förlaget.

Holmström, Mikael, & Tom von Sivers. 1985. *USAs Exportkontroll: Tekniken som Vapen*. Stockholm: Ingenjörsförlaget.

Holmström, Per, & Ulf Olsson. 1983. Sweden. Ball & Leitenberg (1983).

Hufvudstadsbladet. Daily. Helsinki.

Hug, Peter. 1987. *Schweizerische ruestungsindustrie, waffenhandel und friedenspolitik*. December. Mimeographed.

Hug, Peter (ed.). 1988. *Neutrale Weltraumpolitik?* Zürich: Schweizerischer Friedensrat.

Huldt, Bo, & Atil Lejins. 1988. *Neutrals in Europe: Switzerland*. Conference papers, no. 10. Stockholm: Swedish Institute of International Affairs.

Huru, Jouko et al. 1984. *Suomen Asevienti, Jyväskylässä*: K. J. Gummerus.

In Pursuit of Disarmament. 1984a. Part 1A. Background-facts-analyses. Stockholm: Ministry of Foreign Affairs.

In Pursuit of Disarmament. 1984b. Part 1B. Summary-appraisal-recommendations. Stockholm: Ministry of Foreign Affairs.

In Pursuit of Disarmament. 1985. Part 2. Special reports. Stockholm: Ministry of Foreign Affairs.

Inriktningen av säkerhetspolitiken och totalförsvarets fortsatta utveckling. 1977. Government proposition 1976/77, no. 74. Stockholm: Ministry of Defense.

International Defense Review. Monthly. Geneva.

Iran-Contra Affair. 1987. Report of the congressional committees investigating. Washington, D.C.: U.S. Congress. November 17.

Jane's Defence Weekly. Weekly. London.

JAS industrisamverkan. 1986. Report DsI 1986, no. 8. Stockholm: Ministry of Industry.

Jederlund, Lars. 1986. *Kanonekonomi*. Fakta för Fred, no. 6. Stockholm: Swedish Peace and Arbitration Society.

Jennergren, Carl Gustav et al. 1977. *Trends in Planning*. Stockholm: National Defense Research Institute.

Joenniemi, Pertti. 1987. *Finnish arms trade, neutrality and peace*. Paper presented at Varala, Tampere, July 10-12. Mimeographed.

--------. 1989. The peace potential of neutrality. *Bulletin of Peace Proposals* 20, no. 2.

Jones, Barry, & Peter Willetts (eds). 1984. *Interdependence on Trial*. New York: St. Martin's Press.

Jonsson, Bernt. 1985. *The role of the churches in the neutral countries: Some personal notes*. International seminar, Uppsala, November 21-23. Mimeographed.

Journal of Peace Research. 1984. Special issue on alternative defense 21, no. 2.

Kankkonen, Peter. 1979. *Finlandisering – 'Frivillig' Underkastelse*. Uppsala: Pro Veritate.

Karsch, Efraim. 1988. International cooperation and neutrality. *Journal of Peace Research* 25, no. 1.

Kelleher, D.J. 1985. *Security assistance for force modernization: The Saudi Arabian National Guard program*. Student essay. Carlisle Barracks, Penn.: U.S. Army War College. April 15.

Keohane, Robert, & Joseph Nye. 1977. *Power and Interdependence: World Politics in Transition*. Boston: Little, Brown.

Klieman, Aaron. 1985. *Israel's Global Reach: Arms Sales as Diplomacy*. Washington, D.C.: Pergamon-Brassey's.

Kolodziej, Edward. 1979. Measuring French arms transfers. *Journal of Conflict Resolution* 23, no. 2.

--------. 1980. *Arms Transfers and International Politics: The Interdependence of Independence*. Neuman & Harkavy (1980).

--------. 1987. *Making and Marketing Arms*. Princeton, N.J.: Princeton University Press.

Kommittébetänkande. 1981. No. 1. Helsingfors: Parliamentary Defense Committee.

Kosonen, Arto. 1987. *New legal horizons of neutrality and military export: Essays on international law.* Helsinki: Finnish Branch of International Law Association, 1946-1986.

Kranzberg, Melvin. 1969. *Science, technology and warfare: Action, reaction and interaction in the post-World War II era.* Wright & Paszek (1969).

Krigsmaterielinspektionens handbok. 1988. Stockholm: Krigsmaterielinspektionen.

Krigsmaterielinspektionens statistik över svensk krigsmaterielexport. Annual. Stockholm: Ministry of Foreign Affairs (War Materiel Inspectorate).

Kungl. Maj:ts proposition ang. krigsmaterielexport. 1971. Government proposition, no. 146. Stockholm: Ministry of Trade.

Ljung, Bo et al. 1986. *Försvarsindustriella spörsmål.* Report no. A100008-M5. Stockholm: National Defense Research Institute.

Ljung, Bo et al. 1978. *Svensk flygindustri i ett samhällsekonomiskt perspektiv.* Report no. C10097-M3. Stockholm: National Defense Research Institute.

Louscher, David, & Michael Salomone. 1987. *Marketing Security Assistance.* Lexington, Mass.: Lexington Books.

Luif, Paul. 1985. Neutrality and external relations: The case of Austria. *Cooperation and Conflict* 21, no. 4.

Maude, George. 1976. *The Finnish Dilemma.* London: Oxford University Press.

Med förslag till lag om förbud mot investeringar i Sydafrika och Namibia. 1984. Government proposition no. 56. Stockholm: Riksdagstryckeriet.

Medborgarkommissionens rapport om svensk vapenexport. 1988. Report SOU, no. 15. Stockholm: Allmänna Förlaget.

Melman, Seymour. 1974. *The Permanent War Economy.* New York: Simon and Schuster.

Memorandum of Understanding Sweden-Austria. 1974. *Sveriges Överenskommelser med Främmande Makter.* No. 20. June 6.

Memorandum of Understanding Sweden-Switzerland. 1966. *Sveriges Överenskommelser med Främmande Makter.* No. 102. August 4.

Milavnews. (International Air Forces & Military Aircraft Directory Newsletter). Monthly. Romford (Aviation Advisory Services).

The Military Balance. Annual. London: International Institute for Strategic Studies.

Military Technology. Monthly. Bonn.

Milivojevic, Marko, & Pierre Maurer. 1988. The Swiss Army. *Armed Forces 7*, no. 11. November.

Mintz, Alex. 1985. Military-industrial linkages in Israel. *Armed Forces and Society 12*, no. 1.

Moodie, Michael. 1979. *Sovereignty, security, and arms*. The Washington papers, no. 67. Beverly Hills, Calif.: Sage.

Möttölä, Kari. 1984. Finlands Säkerhetspolitik – kontinuitet och nya utmaningar. Andrén (1984).

Mundy, Clare, & Dan Smith. 1980. 'Facts' about the military. *Journal of Peace Research 17*, no. 3.

Murdoch, J.C. & T. Sandler. 1986. The political economy of Scandinavian neutrality. *Scandinavian Journal of Economics*. 88, no. 4.

Nelson, Donald. 1946. *Arsenal of Democracy*. New York: Harcourt, Brace.

Neuman, Stephanie. 1986. *Military assistance in recent wars: The dominance of the superpowers*. The Washington papers, no. 122. New York: Praeger.

Neuman, Stephanie, & Robert Harkavy (eds.). 1980. *Arms Transfers in the Modern World*. New York: Praeger.

Ny Teknik. 50 nos./year. Stockholm.

N-Syntesen. 5-6 nos./year. Stockholm (Nobel Industrier).

Ohlson, Thomas (ed.). 1988. *Arms Transfer Limitations and Third World Security*. Oxford: Oxford University Press.

Olsson, Ulf. 1977. *The Creation of a Modern Arms Industry: Sweden 1939-1974*. Gothenburg: Gothenburg University. Department of Economic History.

Örvik, Karen Erikson. 1979. The limits of security: Defence and foreign trade in Finland. *Survey: A Journal of East & West Studies*, 24, no. 2.

Österrike. 1984. Länder i fickformat. Stockholm: Institute for Foreign Affairs.

Ostrich, John, & William Green. 1981. Methodological problems associated with the IISS Military Balance. *Comparative Strategy* 3, no. 2.

PAX. 8 nos./year. Stockholm (Swedish Peace and Arbitration Society).

Peleg, Ilan. 1977. Arms supply to the Third World - models and explanations. *Journal of Modern African Studies* 15, no. 1.

Pierre, Andrew (ed.). 1979. *Arms Transfers and American Foreign Policy.* New York: New York University Press.

Pillar, Paul. 1983. *Negotiating Peace.* Princeton, N.J.: Princeton University Press.

Pilz, Peter. 1982. *Die Panzermache. Die Österreichische rüstungsindustrie und ihre export.* Vienna: Verlag für Gesellschaftskritik.

--------. 1987. *Austrian arms production and exports.* April. Mimeographed.

PM rörande krigsmateriel vid utförsel och tillverkning. 1966. Memorandum no. 1. Stockholm: Ministry of Trade (War Materiel Inspectorate).

Press Release. 1986. Stockholm: Ministry of Foreign Affairs/Trade. February 27.

Press Release. 1988a. Stockholm: Ministry of Foreign Affairs/Trade. March 3.

Press Release 1988b. Stockholm: Ministry of Foreign Affairs/Trade. April 14.

Rapoport, Anatol. 1960. *Fights, Games and Debates.* Michigan: University of Michigan Press.

Regeringens proposition med förslag till lag om förbud mot utförsel av krigsmateriel m.m. 1982. Government proposition, no. 196. Stockholm: Riksdagstryckeriet.

Regeringens proposition med förslag till lag om förbud mot utförsel av krigsmateriel m.m. 1988. Government proposition no 154. Stockholm: Riksdagstryckeriet.

Regeringens skrivelse med redogörelse för den svenska krigsmaterielexporten. Annual (from 1984). Stockholm: Ministry of Foreign Affairs.

Report of the party working on war materiel export. Summary of main aspects. 1988. Helsinki. Mimeographed.

Resources Devoted to Military Research and Development. 1972. Stockholm: Almqvist & Wiksell.

Richardson, Lewis. 1960. *Arms and Insecurity.* Chicago: Boxwood.

Roberts, Adam. 1976. *Nations in Arms.* London: Chatto & Windus.

Rosen, Stephen (ed.). 1973. *Testing the Theory of the Military-Industrial Complex.* Lexington, Mass.: Lexington Books.

Säkerhets- och försvarspolitiken. 1972. Report SOU 1972, no. 4. Stockholm: Ministry of Defense.

Säkerhetspolitik och totalförsvar. 1976. Report SOU 1976, no. 5. Stockholm: Ministry of Defense.

Säkerhetspolitiken och totalförsvaret. 1981. Report DsFö 1981, no. 1. Stockholm: Ministry of Defense.

Samhällsekonomisk analys av framtida flygplansanskaffning. 1976. Stockholm: Ministry of Defense.

Sampson, Anthony. 1978. *The Arms Bazaar.* London: Hooder & Stoughton.

Schaer-Kern, Beat. 1986. The European neutral corridor: An open westward route for Warsaw Pact forces in war? *Royal United Services Institute Journal* 131, no. 3. September.

Schandler, Herbert et al. 1977. *Implications of President Carter's Conventional Arms Transfer Policy.* Report to the Committee of Foreign Relations. U.S. Senate. Subcommittee on Foreign Assistance of the Committee on Foreign Relations. Library of Congress. Washington, D.C.: Congressional Research Service.

Schellenberg, James. 1982. *The Science of Conflict.* Oxford: Oxford University Press.

Schlesinger, Thomas. 1972. *Austrian Neutrality in Postwar Europe: The Domestic Roots of a Foreign Policy.* Wilhelm Braumüller. Vienna: UniversitätsVerlagsbuchhandlung GmbH.

Schweiz. 1970. Några grundläggande data. Stockholm: Ministry of Foreign Affairs.

Schweiz. 1984. Länder i fickformat. Stockholm: Institute of Foreign Affairs.

Security Assistance Program: Congressional Presentation. Annual. Washington, D.C. (Department of Defense).

Senghaas, Dieter. 1972. *Rüstung und Militarismus.* Frankfurt am Mein: Suhrkamp.

Siegler, Heinrich. (n.d.). *Austria: Problems and Achievements since 1945.* Translation. Nonn: Siegler & Co. KG Verlag für Zeitarchive.

Singer, J. David. 1979. *Explaining War.* Beverly Hills, Calif.: Sage.

Sivard, Ruth Leger. Annual. *World Military and Social Expenditures.* Washington, D.C.: World Priorities.

Sjöstedt, Gunnar. 1977. *The External Role of the European Community.* Swedish Studies in International Relations, no. 7. Westmead: Saxon House.

Sorley, Lewis. 1983. *Arms Transfers under Nixon. A Policy Analysis.* Lexington: University of Kentucky Press.

Stanley, John, & Maurice Pearton. 1972. *The International Trade in Arms.* New York: Praeger.

Steckzén, Birger. 1946. *Bofors, en Kanonindustris Historia.* Stockholm: Esselte AB.

Stein, George. 1989. *Austrian defense policy.* Paper presented at the International Studies Association Conference, London, March 28-April 1.

Stenquist, Bjarne. 1982. Finlands säkerhet. *Försvar i Nutid,* no. 2.

Strategic Survey. Annual. London: International Institute for Strategic Studies.

Strategy Week. Weekly. Washington, D.C.

Störend, Harald, & Carl Salicath. 1986. *Svensk sikkerhetspolitikk og forholdet til Sovjetunionen.* Report no. 99. Oslo: Norwegian Institute for Foreign Affairs.

Sundelius, Bengt (ed.). 1982. *Foreign Policies of Northern Europe.* Boulder, Colo.: Westview.

-------- (ed.). 1987. *The Neutral Democracies and the New Cold War.* Boulder, Colo.: Westview.

Svensk försvarsindustri. 1982. Report no. C10200-M5. Stockholm: National Defense Research Institute.

Svensk industri i utlandet. 1982. Report SOU 1982, no. 27. Stockholm: Ministry of Industry.

Svensk krigsmaterielexport. 1970. Report SOU 1970, no. 63. Stockholm: Ministry of Trade.

Svensk krigsmaterielexport. 1981. Report SOU 1981, no. 39. Stockholm: Ministry of Trade.

Svensk säkerhetspolitik inför 90-talet. 1985. Report SOU 1985, no. 23. Stockholm: Ministry of Defense.

Svensk Sydafrikapolitik. 1984. Report SOU 1984, no. 52. Stockholm: Ministry of Foreign Affairs.

Svenska Dagbladet. Daily. Stockholm.

Sveriges Överenskommelser med Främmande Makter. Annual. Stockholm: Ministry of Foreign Affairs.

Swedish national security policy. 1970. Publication no. 5. Stockholm: Ministry of Defense.

Teknik, industri och försvar inför 90-talet. 1981. Report no. 289. Stockholm: Ingenjörsvetenskapsakademien.

Telubaffären. 1981. Report SOU 1981, no. 48. Stockholm: Ministry of Justice.

Tempus. Weekly. Malmö.

Thayer, George. 1970. *The War Business: The International Trade in Armaments.* New York: Simon and Schuster.

Tidskrift för teknisk information från Flygförvaltningens underhålls-avdelning. Irregular. Stockholm (Air Defense Board).

Totalförsvaret 1982/1987. 1981. Report DsFö 1981, no. 14. Stockholm: Ministry of Defense.

Tubin, Eino. 1978. Vad kan vi lära av Schweiz? *Försvar i Nutid,* no. 5.

Udis, Bernard. 1978. *From Guns to Butter.* Cambridge, Mass.: Ballinger.

--------. 1986. *European conversion experience*. Report prepared for the President's Economic Adjustment Committee, Office of Economic Adjustment, Office of the Assistant Secretary of Defense. Washington, D.C.: The Pentagon.

Upsala Nya Tidning. Daily (except Sundays). Uppsala.

Waffenplatz Schweiz. 1983. Bern: Tagungssekretariat für das Leben Produzieren.

van der Bellen, Alexander et al. 1985. *Rüstungskonversion in Österreich*. Vienna: Bundesministerium für Wissenschaft und Forschung. October.

Vår säkerhetspolitik. 1979. Report SOU 1979, no. 42. Stockholm: Ministry of Defense.

Die Verteidigungsstrategien Schwedens und Finlands. 1984. *Österreisische Jahrbuch für International Politik*.

Vetschera, Heinz. 1985. Neutrality and defense: Legal theory and military practice in the European neutrals defense policies. *Defense Analysis*, 1, no. 1.

Voronkov, Lev. 1984. *Non-nuclear status to Northern Europe*. Moscow: Nauka Publishers.

Waldheim, Kurt. 1973. *The Austrian Example*. London: Weidenfeld and Nicolson.

Wallensteen, Peter. 1973. *Structure and War: On International Relations 1920-1968*. Stockholm: Rabén & Sjögren.

Wehrtechnik. Monthly. Bonn.

Welt, Leo. 1984. Offsets for exports. *National Defense* 69, no. 400. September.

Westander, Henrik. 1983. *Svensk vapenexport till krig*. Fakta för fred, no. 3. Stockholm: Swedish Peace and Arbitration Society.

--------. 1988. *Bofors Svindlande Affärer*. Stockholm: Ordfront Förlag.

Westander, Henrik, & Lars Jederlund. 1985. *Ska Sverige beväpna förtryckare?* Fakta för fred, no 5. Stockholm: Swedish Peace and Arbitration Society.

World Armaments and Disarmament. Annual (SIPRI Yearbook). Cambridge, Mass.: MIT Press (-1977); London: Taylor & Francis (1978-1985); Oxford: Oxford University Press (1986-).

World Military Expenditures and Arms Transfers. Annual. Arms Control and Disarmament Agency. Washington, D.C.: Department of State.

Wright, Monte, & Lawrence Paszek (eds.). 1969. *Science, Technology and Warfare.* Proceedings of the third military history symposium, Office of Air Force History, USAF Academy. Washington, D.C.: GPO. May 8-9.

Wright, Quincy. 1965. *A Study of War.* Chicago: University of Chicago Press.

York, Herbert. 1987. *Making Weapons, Talking Peace.* New York: Basic Books.

Ziegler, Jean. 1978. *Switzerland Exposed.* London: Allison and Busby.

Zinnes, Dina et al. 1976. The Arab-Israeli arms race: An empirical examination. *Jerusalem Journal of International Relations* 2, no. 1.

Index